Sunday Adelaja

The Law of
Difference

Sunday Adelaja

The Law of Difference
©2017

ISBN 978-966-1592-80-2

London, United Kingdom
sundayadelajablog.com

To get results reading this book, you should review it as often as possible. Let the selected fragments inspire you to improve your life. As humans, we have an amazing ability to forget.

Cover Design by Olexandr Bondaruk

The Law of Difference
London, United Kingdom

Contents

PREFACE

The world you live in has deceived us into believing that it is our similarity that is to be celebrated, thereby leading us to want to conform to our environment. Meanwhile, the lesson of creation teaches us that it is rather our difference that is celebrated instead of our similarity.

God seems to derive pleasure from diversity. It is mind blowing to even conceive the idea that no human is completely similar to another, so every single one of the over 7 billion people on the face of the earth today are different. Wow! What a diversity. Yet, this is not the message we get. The impression we all have come to believe is as if we are more of the same with most people in our community and environment. The truth though is that nobody has your eyeballs. Out of the 7 billion people on the earth, your eyeballs are not repeated in anyone.

7 billion is an incredibly big number. 7 billion is a lot. I personally come from a country of close to 200 million people and I know we are a lot. Yet, 200 million is like a drop in the ocean compared to 7 billion. Come to think about it, that there is not a single individual out of that 7 billion that possesses the same features like you. Is God trying to tell us something? Could it be that God is celebrating your uniqueness? Could it be that it is not similarity God is pointing our attention to, but to our difference?

The law of difference, is the title of this book and it is not by accident. It is a known fact that nobody has or possesses the exact same fingerprint as yours. Could that mean God is pointing to your difference and my difference? I am compelled to say yes! It is my hope that at the end of this book you will have more reasons than one to begin to celebrate your difference.

The law of difference is one of the 50 books that I have decided to give to the world as my 50th birthday gift. It was originally written in Russian language. I hope my interpreters and translators did a good job, enough for you to capture the essence of the book. God ahead and celebrate your difference.

For the Love of God, Church and Nation.

Dr. Sunday Adelaja.

Introduction

We often lack honor for each other, but in honor is great power, which we still underestimate. There is **nothing** that honor cannot give us! It can solve any problem and bring answers to any questions. Honor can lead us to glory. My dream is that we really begin to honor each other. It is not enough to honor our elders, which is common practice for many, but it is also important to learn to honor ordinary people, people who have less than us, below us or on the same level with us. We must learn to appreciate and honor each other. We must learn to be happy to see each person and to not pass by without paying any attention to people.

It is important to learn to honor each other, to respect each other. In fact, we need to make honor a culture in our society. How can we do this? How do we make sure that each person is important and special to us, to make sure each person is treated with respect? In order that the culture of honor becomes part of our society we need one very important element; In order that honor flourishes among us, we need to esteem one another, we need to learn the LAW of Difference.

We do not know what honor is until we start to notice the differences in others. If we fail to see the uniqueness of each person, we will pass them by just like furniture, trees, sand or stones, things that we do not even notice. We usually walk past these lifeless objects and they leave no trace in our souls. However, we should never treat our fellow human-beings like inanimate objects. If we with great care, will learn to pay attention to the uniqueness of every individual, no matter how small it may seem to us, we will soon notice what we can honor them for. We can see many reasons for giving them respect. Honoring others will enrich the life of each of us and greatly enhance society.

Practical recommendations for reading THIS book

This book can change your life!

Sometimes while we are reading a book, we decide to apply every life lesson we gain. However, often, after only a few weeks, we have completely forgotten about our intentions. You can have a lot of diverse knowledge in your head, but not use it or live by it. Much of what you will read here, will not be something new for you. The question is, what will you do with the knowledge you gain?

Here are six practical ways that will turn your good intentions into good actions.

1. Read this book several times

While reading the book, often stop to consider its contents. Ask yourself how and when you can use a recommendation. After a detailed study of the book, re-read it every month, giving it a few hours. This book should become your handbook.

2. Read out loud

Reading out loud helps to release in your life the power that stands behind every word. It is not only important that every word be seen, *but also that every word be heard.*

Spoken word has wave nature and when you hear it, it has a modifying effect, causes change on all surrounding objects and subjects. **Therefore, words are important.** Do not neglect the power of words! Do not let the power that is literally physically able to change your life and the circumstances you are in pass you by!

3. Underline and take notes

While reading this book, keep a pen or pencil and a highlighter next to you. Underline individual lines of text and paragraphs. This simple action will increase your ability to remember by three times. Record your thoughts and take notes in the margins or in a notebook. Make this book, *your* book. Underlining makes the book more interesting and in the future, help you to quickly go through it again and focus on the parts that were/are important to you.

4. Re-read the underlined pieces

Underlining and making descriptions help you quickly view the most important issues and fragments of this book. To get results reading this book, you should review it as often as possible. Let the selected fragments inspire you to improve your life. As humans, we have an amazing ability to forget. The only way to save much needed information in your memory is to go back to it repeatedly.

5. Immediately apply the principles learned

The use of what you have learned helps you better understand and remember what was read/heard (as you read it aloud). It is impossible to teach a human-being, they can only learn. This means that teaching is an active process. We learn best when we practice what we are taught. If you want to master the principles in this book, practice them often and at every opportunity. If you do not practice them, then you will very quickly forget them. Only that which is used, remains in the memory.

6. Give priority to what you learn

Select at least one to three points, with which to start. Begin to use them constantly until they become a habit. Practical use of what you gather from this book can be your habit *only* from constant repetition. When you do this, you will begin to apply it automatically, without even thinking about it.

At the end of each chapter you *will* find **golden truths**, which will gather all the important ideas throughout the chapter. Also, you will find **tests procedures** to help assess yourself and your skills along with **practical tasks** *that* will help you make them your lifestyle. **They are not designed just for reading.** To help you get maximum results and benefits from these practical exercises, I advise to execute them within 24 hours, otherwise you will be distracted and forget all about your destiny and purpose. If you distance yourself from taking advantage of these tools you will not see the results you expect.

In my years of experience, I know that people usually perform these kinds of tasks «Superficially». However, you are not in school, where you can get away with all sorts of carelessness, just performing for a grade and not really taking in the lesson. This is about your life and your efforts towards in-depth fulfillment of the tests will determine how your life will change. Therefore, I ask you to take seriously the tasks, as it is not for the author, but for you. To complete the tasks effectively, I advise you to seek quiet place where no one will be able to disturb you. Perhaps it will be a time when there is no one at home, or at night when all are asleep, and no one is able to disturb you.

Be sure to meditate on each chapter, on all the points that you highlighted for yourself, reflect on your decisions and write your follow-up plan of action. Do not forget to schedule specific time periods, determine the restrictions that you impose on yourself. This will help you to not delay the planned steps to change your life forever. Find someone - that you might be accountable to, who may help remind you or partner with you to work on yourselves.

Record the date you began reading and applying this book. Let that date be a new beginning of your life!

Guidelines for the implementation of practical tasks

1. CAUTION: These activities should not only be read and forgotten, they are VERY IMPORTANT. According to many years of working with people I know people often perform such tasks «for the sake of it" but it's your life, this is for you, takethem seriously.

2. To maximize results, I suggest performing the tasks within the 24 hours, otherwise, you will forget, get distracted and you will distance yourself from the results you want.

3. To answer all the questions, find a quiet place and systematically work out the tasks.

4. Meditate on each chapter, on all the points that you underlined for yourself, reflect on the them and write out your steps of action.

5. Set yourself a time frame, constraints, to help you not to put off working on yourself.

6. Find someone you can be accountable to, who could help remind you to stay focused on working on yourself.

How to take tests

Tests that follow each chapter help you analyze yourself and find your true position. Finding your weaknesses, you can strengthen them by using the principles that are presented in this book. Respond honestly and thoughtfully to the test questions; By doing so, you not only help yourself, but also other people with their problems.

In each statement or question in the tests only one answer should be noted. Next to each answer in brackets there is a numeric value for each answer. Your score will determine how ready you are to live out the true values. The tests are not meant to make you feel bad about yourself. Rather, to give you a clear picture of where you are. Each one of us have areas that need to be worked on. By answering honestly, you can gage where you are presently and you can retake these tests during review of the book to track your progress in the future.

Chapter 1

Wisdom sees difference

Wisdom sees differences

One does not understand the smell of roses.
Another from bitter herbs will produce honey.
This one- the detail you give, - remembers forever.
This one- the life you give, and he will not understand.

- Omar Khayyam (1048 - 1131), the Persian poet,
philosopher, mathematician, astronomer, astrologer

Ability to recognize difference... what does this ability imply? It is not so easy to recognize something - it is therefore not so easy to be wise. After all, the ability to recognize something proves the existence of wisdom. Recognizing something is an act of wisdom, and is a confirmation that a person possesses wisdom.

Imagine a situation: in front of you are three tablets. At first glance, they are all the same, since they all look alike: rectangular, plastic, the size of a notebook. At first glance, they are the same thing: what can be the difference between them if all three devices are tablets? But for the person who understands, one who possesses wisdom, one who has some training, it is obvious that they are not the same tablets, there is a difference between them. Through close investigation, you'll find that one of these tablets is manufactured by Samsung, the second - Asus, and the third - Apple. If you understand what you are talking about, you will agree that, despite the resemblance, these are not the same things, right? DISCERNMENT, ABILITY TO SEE THE DIFFERENCE - THAT IS THE PORTION of the WISE[1].

What is wisdom?

A Wise man looked for a capable and talented student, who had the necessary skills and abilities to whom he could pass over his knowledge when he dies. He decided to gather all his students. When everyone gathered, the sage said to them, "I have a problem and would like to know who among you can solve it".

You see: in the wall behind me is the biggest, heaviest and most massive door in the city. Who among you can open it without any help?"

Some students simply lowered their head: the problem seemed insolvable. Others examined the door more thoroughly, discussed the possibility of using a lever and the characteristics of the material and arrived at a conclusion that the problem is impossible to solve. All of them said that to do what the wise man asked is impossible.

Only one student went to the door, and subjected the door to a thorough examination. He tapped the surface of

---

[1] *Soup referred to almost any electronic device*

it, to assess the thickness and density material, he took note of which material it was made and how well the door hinges are lubricated. . He carefully checked it using his eyes and and hands. He pounded on it and pressed on certain areas. Everyone assumed that the door was locked or jammed. And in fact, it was only lightly covered. The student drew a sigh, focused and gently pushed open the door. The Door with ease and without the slightest resistance opened. It was designed and constructed so perfectly that the slightest push was enough to open it.

Sage had found a successor, because the young man had the wisdom to see the difference, where others could not see, as they all tried to «crack» the door. The man who achieved success in comparison to those who failed repeatedly, was distinguished by WISDOM - the ability to see difference. Thanks to wisdom, **those doors that remain closed to most, swing open wide before the wise.** Wisdom reveals to a man the road to where he could not get to, without possessing this quality.

So, **wisdom - is** the ability to:

discern

see the difference

Law of difference - this is one of multiple manifestations of wisdom, which sees difference. Almost everything in this life depends on the law of difference, and therefore the presence or absence of wisdom.

Thanks to our ability to see difference we have everything we have. If you're a man, why are you wearing exactly that shirt (sweatshirt, T - shirt, sweater)? Because that shirt has something different, and you bought it. If you are woman, why are you wearing clothes of a certain color? Because something in it made you like it more than any other color. In the stores, there are a huge amount of goods, so many of them that eyes just run here and there, taking everything in. But you only buy what is *different from* the rest.

Even the perfume or cologne you use, the choice you made was based on the law of difference. The same applies to clothing and shoes that you wear, cosmetics and hygiene products. Are you satisfied with just any shampoo? Will you agree to any proposal? will you put your hands in just about anything? If anything goes for you, why don't you eat dog-food or cat-food for breakfast or dinner? why not wash your hair with shampoo meant for removing fleas? or why not live somewhere in a box under a bridge next to the homeless?

The way our lives look, all that we have, what we possess, is the result of our how much we recognize and act in accordance with the Law of difference. The reason someone does not choose the most beneficial circumstances or things in life, but clearly choose the most unfavorable, is only because they were unable to recognize the best. EVERYONE HAS EXACTLY WHAT HE OR SHE COULD DISCERN.

If we go to an art gallery, looking at a picture, the copy is indistinguishable from the original. But a specialist in this area would easily recognize the difference. The same applies to precious stones. I can hardly tell a fake from a real stone. However, if there is wisdom, if there is an expert, they can immediately identify the difference. Therefore, **one of the most important actions in life - is the ability to see the difference.**

Only the people who are attentive to details can see and embrace difference. *To see difference, you must be meticulous in everything.* For example, if I see a woman with subtle yet masterful make - up, it immediately becomes clear that the person versed in this matter. This means that the lady sees details, she is knowledgeable in this area.

Not everyone is able to see the difference. Why? Because a person is lacking refinement, or either is not putting in effort to develop themselves, not knowledgeable enough or trained enough, having no skills. Being able to see difference is not as simple as it might seem at first glance.

The ability to see the difference – is the ability to make choices

Choice - deciding from a variety of options offered. [1] Making life choices is not always easy. Even to choose between basic things takes wisdom.

No one will argue with the fact that in the world, there are pants, those made for women and those made for men. We can all agree that there is a noteworthy difference in how they are made to fit two different body types. If I write in a certain order numbers: 2 + 4, you need some wisdom to figure out that adds up to 6. If you write 6 - 4, it also requires a certain wisdom to calculate the difference between 6 and 4, which is 2. *The ability to see the difference is a manifestation of wisdom.* In the world, there are illiterate people who can neither read nor write, and for them, these combinations of numbers mean nothing. Some people cannot differentiate between the 6 - 4 and 2 + 4, because they did not take time to acquire wisdom.

For example, one says: «I want to buy a house!» and another specifies: «I want to buy a house by the sea», and the third, «And I near the forest.» One might say: «What's the difference where I buy a house?» But there is a difference: one, does not see all the details and obvious facts, and buys a house in a rush, in the city for example, where there is traffic congestion and noise, and later regrets the rest of his life. However, the one who carefully chooses the place of his house and buys it, will enjoy it and have no regrets. So, the law of difference is very important in this life we live. It factors into every facet of life.

Another example, put on the table four images: chicken, cat, dog and a tree, and you ask the question, «What is out of place in this list? What does not belong in the same category?» The wise person will tell you that tree falls into another category, as it represents FLORA, the rest belong to the category of ANIMALS. Some will not see any difference, will not even notice the difference, this person does not possess wisdom. THE ABILITY TO SEE THE DIFFERENCE - THIS IS WISDOM. **And if people are not able to notice, unable to see difference, then, they lack wisdom.**

I offer you another example. If I lay on the table notes of different denominations of US dollars, $100, $1, $5 and $10. (Just to let you know, all these denominations have one size.) They are all the same size and color, green! Now I ask you a question: what is the difference? Some may see no difference at all, thinking they are just green pieces of paper, all the same size. If you would offer them to choose, they would say, « what difference does it make? They're all the same! « This person might easily choose the $1 bill, even though they could take advantage of $100. We would say that such a person is unintelligent, they are not wise. Why? Because he does not understand, he does not see the value of the dollar bills, he does not see difference between them. If a person acts like this they are not wise, they do not have skills and knowledge in this regard.

Let's complicate the task: I will offer you a choice of 500 Ukrainian hryvnia, 100 US dollars and 1,000 Russian rubles. What do you choose? One might say - «am I a fool? I would choose 1,000 of course! how can I choose 100 or 500? 1000 is clearly more, than 100 or even 500. I'll take 1000! « But what this person does not know is that 1,000

Russian rubles, which they chose, is about 250 hryvnia, and exchange to dollars - it's just about $20. Wow! Instead of 100 dollars this person chose 20. Why could this person make such a mistake? Because they did not know about currencies, they didn't understand, did not have the wisdom to see the difference.

Wisdom – is the ability to distinguish between main and secondary

It was close to New Year. Natalia worried about how to get the right gifts for her friends. After graduation, she lived alone in Kiev, rented an apartment and earned a living by doing manicure for numerous client. I must say that Natasha earned quite well, and this became the subject of her pride. For once - she could afford generous gifts to relatives at home, in Prilukak a town in the Ukraine, where her Mom and Sister (who already had a child), at that time lived. Natasha felt happy to come home to visit with gifts: On one occasion, she left money for a new refrigerator on another she would brought a lot of delicious and expensive food.

Once again: in order not to lose face, when she came to his hometown, Natasha worked hard – even on the weekends to earn money because the more she made the greater the value of her gifts. Her mom was most special to her and it was for her she put in so much hard-work, not sparing her time or money. For three months Natasha could only see her Mom in her mind, because of her working schedule. She usually visits her relatives every month. But now for a few months she had not seen her mother's face, but Natasha consoled herself saying, "just a little hard work, earn a little more money - and the joyful meeting is not far off". She imagined how her Mom would be happy and would excitedly unpack the gifts, how she will be glad she has such a daughter - smart, strong and diligent. Her Mom would be even more proud of her because her goals are always achieved.

Her dreams of that day with her Mom ended abruptly a few days before the New Year, December 28, Natasha was called and told that her Mother was dead. It sounded to her like a bolt from the blue, such shocking and unexpected news. Why all this effort to make more money? Why all these maneuvers, when the one for whom all the sacrifice was made is no longer alive? Natasha suddenly felt deeply hurt and sorry by the fact that she did not use the opportunity to see her Mother over the last few months, but instead postponed her visit, collecting money for the expensive gifts that no one needs now nor will have opportunity to enjoy.

This girl can be understood in that trying to please her Mother, she missed the most valuable thing that was available to her: time spent with her Mom. Instead of enjoying dynamic conversation with relatives and friends, she had focused her attention on how to supply material needs. Instead of visiting her Mother alive and healthy for a Mother nothing is more precious than to hug her child but Natasha was busy about doing what was important but not the main priority. In the pursuit of success and prosperity, an attempt to give her family and friends what she herself thought they wanted from her, she failed to see the difference between major and minor.

As we said above, **wisdom** is to differentiate, to see the difference. But even this is not enough. We need to learn to see nuances, differentiate them from one another[2]:

good and evil

the main and secondary

significant and insignificant

The ability to see the difference between main and secondary determines the decision a person takes. *Thus, a person's decision is based on their ability to see differences between important and unimportant.*

There is a difference even between important things: my hair-do is important, but if I need to choose between my hand and my hair-do, I will choose my hand and sacrifice my hair-do. My hand is important, but if the issue will be: to amputate a hand or stay alive, I will better sacrifice my hand, because my life is more important than my hand. In the same way, my leg is important, but my head is more important. My hand is important, but not as

---

[2] *Nuances -barely noticeable transition from one to the other way.*

much as my life, I can live without a hand, but what's the need of the hand if I died? My nails are important, but not as much as my heart, you can live without nails or without fingers, but not without a heart. There are major important things and minor.

This is the reason why we need to learn to distinguish: Hair-do is important, but the hand is more important. Make-up is needed and important, but if you are confronted with the option: stay alive and do not use make-up, then I think you will agree, to stay alive is a better decision, right?

A beautiful woman, an actress was engaged in advertising, so that every day we could see her on TV. She was in great demand by the directors because of her hair: the nature of her hair was surprisingly rich and luxurious. But when the actress fell ill with cancer, the first thing that was sacrificed in the fight against the disease – was her hair. As you know, sessions of chemotherapy – is a pretty tough test, not only for the body but for the mind, especially for women, whose ornament has always been the hair. Imagine how valuable hair is for the woman! Not only that, her hair had been a subject of pride, it was also an important part of her professional success. However, for the sake of her life the actress agreed to sacrifice her hair.

We must learn to discern what is important in life, there are - the important thing, but there may be - some things that are more substantial. Sometimes you do not need to rush into a fight because it is not worth it. Sometimes it is more appropriate to close your eyes to trivial things, just let it go, it's not worth the fuss. As an illustration, let me offer you a wise parable about how to react to insults and envy of others.

Once upon a time, lived one wise old samurai. He had a group disciples, whom he taught the wisdom of life. One day in class, he was approached by a young soldier, who had a reputation for being impolite and cruel man. As a tactic, he used provocation: first he insulted the enemy, ensuring that he lost his temper and rushed into the fight. The hope was that in a rage, having lost self -control, the enemy will make a range of mistakes, as a result, the enraged enemy would then be defeated.

With respect to the wise old samurai the young warrior tried to apply the same technique back at him. He threw some abusive remarks, watching the reaction of the latter. The wise old samurai calmly continued his studies with his students. This was repeated several times. Failing to get a response, the young soldier went away in a rage.

Those other students were watching the scene. When the soldier left, one of them could not hold himself back, so he asked his mentor:

- "Master, why did why you tolerate all this? Why did you not take him on in a fight?"

To this the wise samurai gave an answer:

- *"If you are offered something, but you do not accept it, who does it belong to?"*

- *"the former owner" – replied the students.*

- *The same goes for envy, hatred or insults. AS LONG AS YOU DO NOT TAKE THEM, THEY BELONG TO THE PERSON WHO BROUGHT THEM.*

Sometimes it is not necessary to answer the attacks of the enemy. Sometimes it is wiser to remain silent than engage in open confrontation and start a fight. And again, here, just as in life, you need to be able to understand that there are **very important issues and not very important, so you must discern the value of what we are now discussing.** Work is important, but perhaps even more important is relationship with others? Making money is important, but maybe an expression of care to parents is more important? I'm important, but perhaps without other people I won't amount to anything? **ONLY WISDOM ALLOWS YOU TO SEE DIFFERENCE.**

Everything is relative

What is at stake all depends on the price of the issue. In ordinary life, we can hardly get over a fence several feet high, it may seem impossible to us. However, when there is a real threat to human life many people demonstrate real miracles: raising very heavy objects to release a child trapped underneath it, jumping over very high barriers, etc. You might think that you can never leave your work, but if your baby's health is threatened and they have been taken to the hospital, then you will go to any length to be close to the child, to care for him or her. **WE UNDERSTAND THINGS BETTER IN COMPARISON.** It is important to focus or put emphasis on the right things, never say: « *I would never do that!* » You do not know where you will find yourself or what situation you will be in one day. **Everything in life is relative, therefore it is important to see difference: what is important today, can lose its value and cease to be important tomorrow. That which was unimportant yesterday, forgotten and corrupted, can become relevant today. It can acquire a new meaning filled with new understanding and significance.**

Always take advantage of the moment, learn to appreciate while there is still time to appreciate, to make use of what is available, to take advantage of what you can use. For this reason, do not neglect any moment, not one moment that you get. Different times create different questions: what is not quoted yesterday can become the leading trend today. And in this way also the Law of difference expresses itself. Do not be rigid about something in life - try to look at the difference and understand what is needed now. What is valuable in the present moment.

Do what you can do now, use the moment that is at your disposal. To take advantage of the "big moment", you need to learn to discern, to see difference. Appreciate your Mother, take care of her, while there is time, because tomorrow may be too late. Help your Mother, not putting off what you can do today, with the excuse that life is very hard for you too. Often our relatives do not need a lot: one flower, an extra phone call, small gifts like chocolate bars. To wait while you try to earn all the money possible to earn, may be too late. Those who you desired to enjoy all the fruits of your labor, may no longer be alive. People cannot wait forever for your arrival, while you are busy trying and preparing to surprise them with another gorgeous gift. Learn how to discern the difference in time, appreciate the time and those moments that you already have.

Sometimes women look at their husbands and think, «He is awkward, ridiculous, a clown!» But when the husband is suddenly on the verge of death, then the woman begins to realize she will never see him again, then a reassessment of the events of their life together sets in. The woman suddenly begins to ask herself: «why did I scream at him? Why did I not answer when he called? Why did I refuse him, when I did not really have a headache? ». All his

deficiencies that so irritated her suddenly become insignificant, and in the fore front comes those things which she did not see or appreciate. When the husband is no more, almost all wives are ready to do anything if only their husband was still there. Ask any widow, and she will tell you that she had, in general, a good husband. Why did she then complain all the time during his lifetime? «then I didn't understand …», would be her response. **LIFE IS A MOMENT THAT SHOULD BE APPRECIATED. Even the opportunity to live life with another person is a chance that should be appreciated and you should be grateful for.** A person who has agreed to live with you, should be honored. Here is yet another manifestation of the Law of difference that in the hustle and bustle of daily life, we sometimes do not consider and do not notice.

We were told that our hair is important but not as important when we need to save the hand. Now imagine that your child has spoiled your hair. What is your reaction? I think that some would be ready to kill the child. You know that if the life of your child was in danger, you would be ready to give ALL your hair, just to save them. Then why would you then scold the child for messing up your hair?

A family of immigrants from Ukraine, moved in the 1980's to America, lived comfortably: had a spacious and comfortable house, car, promising work. The Father was proud of his seven children and the youngest, a long-awaited son was born. The only son was the pride of his Father.

One would say, they were living a happy life. There were no signs of problems.

The Father had a favorite «toy», a car, that he had always dreamt of having. He was so attached to his «iron horse», he could not take his eyes off it, idolizing and cherishing his car. One day, when the man was engaged in minor repairs, he briefly had to go into the house, leaving the tools by the car. His 6 year-old son, was near the unattended car. Like any kid, wanting to play with mechanical things, he grabbed one of the tools of his Father and with all the force he could gather began to beat on the hood of the car. Apart from interest in mechanical things, boys usually experience cravings to test their physical strength, trying to break or crush things, anything in sight. This time the boys' hand was on his father's car.

As we know, it was not just a car, but a vehicle for the family. The Father hearing the noise began breathing unevenly, out of tender feelings for his «baby» on four wheel. Finally, he appeared from the house, the car's hood already damaged by the efforts of his young son. The Father's feeling became out of control, the angry man grabbed the child's hand and began to beat on it with the same wrench which had become the instrument of barbaric action by his boy. He beat his child several times no longer able to control himself. At the end, the hand of the child turned into one big mess. When the Father realized what he was doing, it was too late.

At the hospital where the boy was finally hospitalized, it was decided his hand had to be amputated because it was impossible to salvage. When the child saw his Father, his eyes full of pain, asked, «Dad, when will my hand rise again?». The Man, unable to bear the pain of what he had done, in great inner turmoil he committed suicide.

Such tragedies are result of lack of understanding of the law of difference. The boy became a cripple, his father died, leaving his wife a widow and seven orphaned children. **When we fail to discern, what is valuable at a moment, we can make fatal mistakes.**

Where does lack of wisdom lead?

THE INABILITY TO SEE DIFFERENCE DEPRIVES US OF WISDOM.

Lack of wisdom blinds us and we lose the ability to **see:**

what can be learned?

what can I take away from this?

how can this enrich me?

For example: the inability to see the difference between two different girls, can lead to an assumption that there is nothing remarkable in either of the girls. It would be impossible to appreciate the values in these girls if we cannot see *their difference, originality, and uniqueness.*

Being engulfed only with oneself, a person loses the gift of wisdom, and becomes a fool. WHERE WE DO NOT SEE DIFFERENCE, WE ARE BLIND. If we do not see difference, it is not because there are none, but because we are blind in this area. *In all areas, wisdom looks for difference, stresses and honors them.*

Let's return to our example of the money. Anyone who discerned that all the bills were green, all the same size, but out of all them, the $100 bill was the best option, is already at a certain level of wisdom. This man knows math and was guided by comparing the numbers, he discerned which one was more and which one was less. However, if in the example a person decides to opt for the 1,000 Russian rubles, following the same principle that: the best option is when you choose largest numbers - then this would be an unwise choice. That person did not bother to see the difference, and when he was offered a different currency, he responded only to the largest number: 1,000. We must discern difference, we must be able to see that 1,000 Russian rubles is much less than 500 hryvnia, even much less than $100.

All these examples are about the ability to see difference, the ability not only to differentiate between money, but also to know the value each of the currencies represented. In the first instance the correct answer would be the money with the biggest number, in the latter it was necessary to understand the value of the currencies of different countries. To this end, you must know more, see deeper, have a subtle understanding of the issue, wisdom is needed. **If a person does not have wisdom, they will never be a winner!**

Now let's consider more serious questions. Some people get married and still manage to get into a mess. This is not because they are worse than others or unlucky. I do not advocate that there are those who are lucky in life, and there are those who are not lucky. I think that if anyone – is "lucky in life", it is only because the person was prepared, they «did their homework,» they prepared for the arrival of success in their lives. I do not think that those who crashed in the construction of their family life are worse than others. If out of five girlfriends, three got married and divorced, I do not think that these three are worse than the other two. That they divorced is just because they probably overlooked something. «Overlooked» means they did not see concrete difference.

Anyone who chooses a wife should see some differences: How is she different from others? What distinguishes her from other women, whom he did not see as his life's companion? The one who selects a husband should also know what differentiates this man from all others, she did not see as her husband. If one chooses a life-partner superficially, out of those who happen to be close and does not study and did not list out the difference in the partners, then this neglect can later lead to permanent damage or disappointment.

Also, if a person chooses a husband only by two categorical parameters, for example, fair-haired and tall or blue-eyed and slender, etc., then this kind of approach provides very little ground for success. One needs a more quantitative and qualitative detailed list of qualities, analyzing the candidate using many different parameters, to discern his or her difference that corresponds to your desired requirements. Many people do not do an in - depth analysis, they do not look at that what distinguishes that person from all other people, and therefore fail in their attempt to start a family.

A lot in life depends on the availability of wisdom, the ability to see difference. If you have three children, and you do not see the difference between them and you try to bring them up the same way, then you will fail miserably, just because you did not consider the unique differences of each child.

Let's look at the following scenario. A person went to the store to buy food, because they were asked to buy apples, potatoes and cabbage. A person without wisdom may say: *«What's the difference? They are all products, I will use all the money to buy sausages!»*. Without considering that apart from sausages there is chicken and many different types of meat and fish. To give away all the money on sausage would not be wise at all. Why? Because such a person did not consider the law of difference, they do not see that their diet should be made up of variety of food products. No matter how tasty sausage may be, even if it's your favorite product, you cannot live for a long time on just sausages. Even if you try this, the organ you are trying to fill with food will punish you with indigestion and bad health.

In 2004, a stunning film «Super-Size Me» by film director and actor, Morgan Spurlock, examines the fast food industry of the mega corporation McDonald's. Spurlock created a great documentary, risking his own health.

The film has two distinct plot that connects one topic. The first tells the story of how Morgan Spurlock decides to conduct an experiment in which for a month he is eating only products from McDonald's. The second story contains unique statistical and analytical data; Surveys of people consuming products from McDonald's.

Spurlock whose weight during the experiment increased by 24 pounds, decided to show fans what could occur by only eating fast food for 30 days. Many indicators of health got worse. Numerous experts, which consulted with Spurlock: a cardiologist, a gastroenterologist, a nutritionist, all of them had well - founded concerns about his experiment. In spite of everything, he completed the experiment[3]

Morgan Spurlock's experiment showed that a continuous diet of fast food from restaurants, is causing great harm to health. During this 30 days of fast food at McDonald's:

- *gained 24 pounds*

- *liver was in a terrible state (fat in his liver)*

- *2 - fold increase in risk of heart attack*

- *blood sugar and cholesterol levels rose to very high levels*

---

[3] *FAST Food (eng. FAST « fast » and food « food «) with reduced power уменьшенным Management device and приготовления, with simplified and the Abolition of cutlery or off the table.*

- *began to develop sexual dysfunction and physical weakness*

- *experienced depression and food addiction*

The experimental results confirmed the Morgan Joint Study conducted by researchers from New Zealand, Spain, UK, Germany and Australia, which reveal that fast food products have a negative impact on human immune systems and bodies.

The study involved nearly two million children of all ages from more than 100 countries. During the study, the children who ate fast food more than three times a week were significantly more susceptible to diseases such as allergies, asthma, atopic dermatitis and allergic rhinitis. Their liver and cardio - vascular systems operated with significant deviations from the norm. According to scientists, this is because in the production of fast food contains a huge amount of saturated fatty acids, trans fats and sugar. Too much of these substances in the human diet can severely disrupt the body's immune system and undermine health. [2]

Is this not impressive information? This tells us about the value of wisdom. About the wisdom that we need every day, even when you select food for yourself or your children. Lack of wisdom here may result not only in loss of physical health, but also pose a threat to life. The quality of life can fall sharply, so think about how to make wise choices in your life, even when it comes to food. Don't let convenience send you down a wrong path of eating. When there is no wisdom, the man does not see the difference. However, wisdom allows you to see the differences. **Only the wise man - the one who has learned to see the differences - can make the right choices.**

I invite you, dear reader, to draw conclusions on this chapter

1. To live according to the Law of differences, enough to be a wise man

2. With wisdom, we can distinguish between main and secondary

3. Almost everything in this life depends on the law of differences and the presence or absence of wisdom

Well, here we are at the end of the first chapter of this book. In it, we discovered that **WISDOM SEES DIFFERENCE!** But this is the first condition to live by the law of difference. In the next chapter, we will talk about the principles of the law of difference. We will learn, how we need to see advantages in others, to see the dignity of people and that we need to read people. See you in the next chapter, dear reader!

GOLDEN TRUTHS

To understand the law of difference, we need wisdom

Being engulfed with only themselves, people lose the gift of wisdom, and become foolish

Where we do not see difference, we are blind

Wisdom - is the ability to discern, to see difference

With the help of wisdom those doors that remain closed for most people will swing wide open for the wise

If a person is not able to see difference, then they do not possess wisdom

The ability to see the difference between the main and the secondary determines which decision a person makes

What is at stake all depends the price of the question

There are high priority and not high priority questions, so it is important to discern what the value of what we are discussing

SELF – ASSESSMENT

1.Can you distinguish between main and secondary, important and insignificant?
    1) No (0)
    2) Not always, 50/50 (1)
    3) Yes (2)

2.Do you feel the need for wisdom?
    1) No (0)
    2) Partly (1)
    3) Yes (2)

3.What caused the decisions that you make?
    1) I never thought about it (0)
    2) Short - term interests or problems (1)
    3) How it can impact my life on the long-term (2).

EVALUATION OF TEST RESULTS

(0 points) Unfortunately, the level of your wisdom is poor. You hardly see the difference between completely different things, you do not notice the difference when they are obvious. This complicates your life and takes away your

chances for the success that you have been waiting for, if you had in detail, followed the law of difference. To help correct the situation, further detailed study of all the chapters of this book is necessary. It is NEVER too late to acquire wisdom!

(1 - 5 points) Not bad! You have the will to acquire wisdom to a greater extent. You seek to know all the finer details, features and differences. You crave to see the difference where it is needed. If you will do this, life by the Law of the difference will bring you more prosperity and will help you reach a new level of life. So do not be stingy in your efforts to dig deeper and to know more details and nuances about the law of difference. This book will help you: read it, follow all the practical activities and practice the knowledge acquired. Then success undoubtedly awaits you!

(6 points) We can congratulate you! You are approaching a high level of wisdom, so that you are almost deserving the title of a leading figure in this sphere. Living by the law of difference will help you quickly get up to the next level of success in your life. The law of difference will help you be fulfilled in life, but as you advance in it, do not forget about others - share with them your talents and skills. Your wisdom will help many people attain success in life!

Guidelines for the implementation of practical tasks

1. *CAUTION: These activities should not only be read and forgotten, they are VERY IMPORTANT. According to many years of working with people I know people often perform such tasks «for the sake of it» but it's your life, this is for you, take them seriously.*

2. *To maximize results, I suggest performing the tasks within the 24 hours, otherwise, you will forget, get distracted and you will distance yourself from the results you want.*

3. *To answer all the questions, find a quiet place and systematically work out the tasks.*

4. *Meditate on each chapter, on all the points that you underlined for yourself, reflect on the them and write out your steps of action.*

5. *Set yourself a time frame, constraints, to help you not to put off working on yourself.*

6. *Find someone you can be accountable to, who could help remind you to stay focused on working on yourself.*

Practical tasks

What is wisdom? how do you understand it? What are the characteristics of wisdom? How does wisdom help to live according to law of difference?

Examine your life and basic specific facts of life, answer the following questions: What factors influenced your choice? What prevented you from making the right choice? What are you guided by when making choices in your life:

in the acquisition of food, clothing, household items, furniture, real estate, transport, insurance?

in building a career?

in the choice of education (schools, university, other educational institution)?

in your personal life when choosing a future spouse?

Based on the results of the analysis, record what mistakes you made in the exercise of choice. How can they be avoided in the future? Using available experience to develop a system of decision - making, which you can use in the future.

Chapter 2

Principles of the law of difference

Principles of the law of difference

So, dear reader, I greet you in the new chapter of the book entitled «The Law of Difference». The previous chapter was devoted to the wisdom in that aspect that wisdom sees difference. Through reliable study we understood that the ability to see difference is the ability to make right choices. We also found out for ourselves that wisdom is the ability to distinguish between major and secondary, because everything is relative! Finally, we have learned the consequences of lack of wisdom.

Learning about wisdom we did not stop talking about the law of difference. Because if we were living under the law of difference, we would be looking at the difference in the people around us, only wisdom seeks and eventually finds difference. **To understand the law of difference, we need wisdom.** Only wise people know and live by the law of difference. When there is no wisdom, a person does not see difference, and even if he sees it, he does not see the «star» in others. To recognize the «star» in the other person, we also need wisdom. Only wise people can recognize the significance in others. More on this will be discussed in the sixth chapter.

We need to understand that the law of difference is a law that you need to learn in order to live. For this one must learn to:

- *see the advantages of other people*

- *notice the difference of other people*

All this is needed on the long-run to:

- *learn*

- *imitate*

- *to be transformed into the likeness of the person we value*

What is in fact, the law of difference? It is that everyone should understand that everyone, I SEE, every person on this earth was created by God and is unique, and every person on this earth has one thing better than me. I think this news is not pleasant, especially for women. I am sure that many of you, dear women, do not want to recognize the fact that someone is better than you. I can just hear some women's conversation: «No, only I'm beautiful! .....Only I am better than everyone!». Practically almost all women want to be the only and the most beautiful, but it's not true! There will always be someone who has something that is not in you. In some other woman is exactly that which you lack. *Each person on this earth possesses something, that I do not have. We must learn to look at the world only from this point of view.* When we look at ourselves like: « *I am the only one!* », this is a direct path to a psychiatric hospital.

How often do we look at people?

Most often, we look at a person seeking what is worse in that person than in us, so that we can see ourselves in a more favorable light in the background of the other person. For example, *«he, too is wearing a suit, but I am younger, I'm stronger. Uh Oh, his hair is already gray, almost all bald, he is a decrepit old man, but I, I am much better, I am much younger than him! »* If we look at a person with disdain: *«...so young! What can she teach me? »*, etc., then this means that we do not see difference. If we look at a person, we are not looking down on the person but on us in the first place, and we lose where we could have been enriched.

Our human nature pushes each of us to ensure that we do not perceive people in terms of their dignity or advantages but rather in terms of our benefits: **how much better we are, or how we can look in a more favorable light.** It follows from this thesis: our perception of others is based:

Either on the fact that we see the shortcomings of others

or on what we can learn from this person

So, it's either one of these **two things: either we look for shortcomings, or we will look for value, for dignity, for advantages.** Most people tend to notice first defects. Not in any country of the world have I seen such an attitude towards people as in the countries of the former Soviet Union: here people tend to notice and see disadvantages and the negatives in people. In the West, this trend is already being overcome, particularly in America, there, people tend to look for, and notice the positives or advantages of a person. In some instances, even if we see the obvious advantages of a person, other people refuse to notice them. People will carefully search out the negatives that are deeply hidden on the inside. It is against this attitude tendency we must direct our fight.

We must learn to notice the advantages of people first not their disadvantages. . If we have seen the benefits of a person, then, we have positioned ourselves to becoming their disciple, we can learn from them. If we see the flaws and weaknesses, then we become judges. Life is such, that there is always someone who knows what you do not know, and certainly we can find someone whose help you might need in the future. If we are only looking for flaws in others, then we destroy and tear apart relationships with people. If we seek dignity, we are looking for how to gain what this person has, what they know and what we do not have. If we discover the advantages of others, we run after them, we ask them questions, we make them understand that they are special to us, we honor them, then we do not wonder, asking what we can learn from them, we value them.

So, there exists only two ways we can look at people either to condemn or to learn from them, and the second is much better.

How we need to look at each person?

Each person I meet is superior to me in something, and in this sense I can learn from him.

- Ralph Waldo Emerson (1803 - 1882), American writer, poet and philosopher; One of the thinkers and writers of the United States

Let me ask you the following question, dear reader, what do you think? when we see a person, how should we relate to him or her? I want to tell you that there are two ways how we can relate to people:

1. **We take a person as created in the image of God,** and because of this truth they are worthy of respect, or

2. **We look at them and humiliate them,** thinking, «I am wearing a suit, and he who are they? What a strange person, perhaps, a drug addict... »

If I look at a person the way as described in number two, "aha, they are just a former drug addict..., etc." then I can never honor such a person. I have already set myself above that person and this is a manifestation of arrogance and vain glory: «I'm so elegant, and he - who is he?» and inside of me I cannot honor such a person. The truth is that we must **look at every person as the one who can enrich us.** Here is the correct position which we should take in relating to others: "anyone can enrich me!".

When we look at a person as someone that is (in something) «*superior to me*», as Emerson stated, as a person who is above us, better in something than us, when we do not despise him in our heart, then the wealth in this person can enrich us. «*I can learn from him or her*». Only when we look at a person with respect, we set free what they have into our lives, we become their disciple and can learn from their wisdom and knowledge.

Each person knows something I do not know and so I bow before them and always stay in a position of hunger to learn; to be ready to receive their experience and be enriched with the knowledge that they have. Only when you honor and respect others, can you be open to receive and take what they have, you can add to what you have, that which they have. Only when you recognize that they have something that you do not have, they know something you do not know, only then can you take from them.

If someone can do something better or more than us or possesses that which we do not have the law of difference demands that we honor that person, no matter who he or she may be. If we notice their benefits, we can admit that we either do not have or we have less of what we see in that person, therefore, this pushes us to agree to learn from these people. People that do not want to learn from anyone, they only want others to learn from them, they believe they already know everything.

We must recognize a person, even if we perceive the person is worse than us. Remember that we can learn from the example of others. Altogether it's not good to look at people thinking we have something better than them. We must always look at people from the standpoint of what we can learn from them. Never look down on people, always look up to them, from the position of what we can learn from these people. We need to look at all people just like a student would look at the teacher!

When I meet with anyone, I kneel down. In my heart, I am humble and respectful, and with this attitude, I always make a person feel as if he is bigger than he or she is in reality. Who has ever met me, or had fellowship with me, must have noticed that I always try to make a person bigger than they really are and this is the impression they leave with after meeting with me. It means that I voluntarily humble and belittle myself, to honor the people.

And therein lies the art of love for people. This is what God requires of us: *love God "AND» your neighbor.* This means that we must look at that person as someone who knows what we do not know, someone we can learn from, because they are unique, have unique experiences, unique skills, unique talents and gifts. We should not only see that a person is different from us, but we should see each person, as if falling on our knees, this is important! We need to meet every person as if bowing in front of them, already on our knees, we are in the position of a pupil. Each person has something to learn and something worth emulating. When we seeing a person, are inclined to hear what they have to say, and to learn from them and the wisdom they possess: this is what I call «treat others with respect» or «taking them highly, treating them with dignity.»

How to learn to see the difference of human beings?

There is enough light for those who want to see, and enough darkness for those who do not.

- Blaise Pascal (1623 - 1662), engineer, physicist, philosopher

Starting with the argument that all people around us are worthy of some honor, I would like us to see the principle which Blaise Pascal talked about. He spoke about the fact that we will always have enough power and resources to see what we want to see but if we do not want to see something in people, we will find any explanations and justifications (DARKNESS) why we did not see them.

ONLY WHERE WE SEE DIFFERENCE ARE WE ENRICHED

- *Just what we see as unique enriches us*

- *Only from that source, where we see the uniqueness, we can get something useful*

- *Just what we see as difference can be a valuable tip and help us in our lives*

But where we neglect the uniqueness and differences of others, we are missing what could be our wealth. Every time when you can see any person remember, he or she probably knows something that you do not know.

You cannot be enriched in dialogue with the person in which you do not see difference, where the person is better or greater than you. You should see the value they represent and can share with you. They will never be able to enrich you, if you do not see the difference, how they are different from you. **ONLY THE ONE WHO IS UNLIKE US IS A HUGE VALUE FOR US.**

For example, my wife can give me valuable advice on family life, pregnancy and parenting, because she has already passed this way. Her unique expertise is her difference, and thanks to this, she can become for me the person who opens my eyes to see many things unknown to me. If I need advice on how not to go the path of addiction, then who is in a better position to help me, than the person who has experienced this personally? The bitter experience of the addicted person is their distinction, and if I admit it, then they can enlighten me on this issue. How can a husband deal with a sick, bedridden wife who cannot have understanding any of what is being said, is she simply intolerable? I have not passed this way, but the husband of such a woman knows deeply well, first-hand what it's all about and only from such a person, I can get the answer to all my questions, If I were to be in a similar situation.

If I see difference in a person: in whatever sphere their difference is in comparison to me, wherever they are superior to me, have advantages, where they are richer than me, those are the areas I can turn to that person for advice and help. However, if I just know this person, but do not see them as a source of valuable knowledge and wisdom for myself, if I do not see their wealth and resources that could be useful to me, then I would ignorantly despise what could have been a great help to me and would not in such a case turn for help where my help really is, where my questions could genuinely be answered.

We often think that our life is hard. I know a woman who lives without both legs. She uses artificial limbs, yet gave birth to a daughter, brought up the child and she lives without a husband. If you need to encourage someone or you need a source of encouragement, how to live without excuses, then go to her and ask how she can live without two legs, never complaining. How could she live like this without complaining about anything? How could she live like this without grumbling and hating the whole world, not cursing the whole world, but rather enjoying life? If I can see the difference in that woman, her experience would enrich me. However, if I do not see her difference, I deprive myself of the lessons she has acquired through wisdom.

Whatever a person is, even if they are homeless and I believe that I am better than they are, I absolutely cannot to look at them from a different perspective. Even when

I clearly see myself in all respects superior to that person, then I look at this situation from the side, namely: *how can I help that person?* In general, this situation can be described as follows: we are leaders for someone, instructors to someone, people who are older, better, wiser. So, when we are clearly superior to the others, when it is obvious that we understand more, we see further and deeper, it is forbidden to look down on others. When we understand what they are not able to understand, when we see how we can help these people, the only thought which is right, is: « *how can I help this person?* ».

Often, we observe people who live on the street. All is well with us but these people are in very poor conditions. When I'm faced with this situation, I start asking myself questions about my responsibility to this person, my human responsibility, the responsibility God imposes on me as more powerful socially. I remind myself that standing before me, is a human created in the image and likeness of God, who does not have much of what I have. So how can I help? How can I improve their life? Perhaps I can tell them something sensible? How can I give assistance: share with them a gracious smile, take them in my arms to give warmth and love, welcome them, let them know that I see them, that they are not invisible to me? How can I somehow improve their life? What can I offer?

Asking yourself these questions and working out a chain of responses that will then find continuation in my following actions, in this way I will destroy from the roots any reason for arrogance and pride. I will improve myself, working on my heart and attitude to people. I will not remain cold and insensitive to the people around me, not even interested in their fate. I will not run past those who need help, driving them away like annoying flies. I will not close my eyes to the needs of people, staying blind and deaf to their silent screams and moans of pain. Then I will get rid of the callousness that wants to take residence in my heart. I will not let my soul be covered with tight impenetrable scab of indifference. I think this allows me to remain human and not become a soulless animal, concerned only with my problems and needs.

When we are concerned to genuinely help someone instead of admiring ourselves and humiliating others compassion and understanding is awakened. This makes our heart better, purer and nobler. And the best way to do it is to take responsibility for something, to do something concrete to help those weaker than we are find ways how to make their lives easier.

Why do we need to honor people?

Do not work on the other people, work on your thoughts about the other people.

- Robert Kiyosaki (b. in 1947), entrepreneur, writer, lecturer

With the ability to see difference in others, we can honor them. If I do not see a reason I can honor a person, I will pass by them. So, why do we need to honor other people? I want to tell you, dear reader, there is always something to honor in all humans. Each person that you see knows something you do not know. Each person can enrich you, even those I teach, can know about something more than me. Why? Because the person lived in another family unlike me, so they have some experience that I have not had. They heard from their parents, from their neighbors, something I had never heard. I did not live on the street where they lived, I did not live in the family where they grew up. I did not go to the school from which they graduated, I did not read the books they read, I did not work there where they worked. Even if you do not know the specific circumstances of any person, you should always keep in mind the following: a person has had experience, which I do not have, they overcame and took tests that I did not. Because of all the above reasons, we can conclude that everyone has unique experiences and for this reason they are valuable to me and worthy of my respect. Every person is worthy of respect from my part!

When interacting with people if we only think of ourselves, think about how we are better than others are, then we have taken a position of superiority, arrogance, and this will prevent us from respecting the person. If we look at a person and see them as inferior to us, then we cannot revere them. If we approach other people from the position of «I'm better,» or «I'm more beautiful", or «I'm better dressed,» we will not be able to appreciate worth. In the ancient treasury of wisdom, the Bible, an interesting statement that can be found *«honor all, love the brotherhood, fear God, honor the king»*. There are different gradations, different levels of human relationships. There is a vertical relationship with earthly authority «Honor the king» vertical relationship with heavenly authority, «Fear God", respect and attend with reverence to His word. There are also horizontal relationships with people, equal to us, «love the brotherhood". The crown of it all is a terrific word «Honor all!». This means that all have something for which they can be honored.

We often shrug off the people, "was a drug-addict, was an alcoholic, was homeless", and we think that this is a reason to despise the person. This is not true, everything **others have, that we do not have, whether positive or negative experiences is the cause and reason for respect and reverence for them.** I repeat: if a person went through something, through which they acquired some experience .

Napoleon Hill (1883 - 1970), the American author in the area of new thoughts, one of the creators of the modern genre, SELF-HELP, said something very important to understand, why we need to honor other people: *«every negative event carries the embryo of goodness»*. We can easily derive helpfulness from positive experience. It is much more difficult extracting this embryo of goodness either from someone else's or our own personal life. This is possible nevertheless and we need to keep our focus in life on doing that.

God is my witness: not one person do I look down on with contempt or neglect. I always remind myself that someone knows something that I do not know. How do I know this? Quite simply, no matter how a person is, they might have lived on the street where I did not live, which means he went through some life circumstances that I did not go through. Even if the person is a former drug addict, that is their difference which gives me the reason to honor him. Why? Because they went through something that I did not to go through, something that I never came across in my life. And I must bow before this man and see what I can learn from him, I must remove my hat before him. The fact they were a drug addict is not a reason to have arrogance or pride. Who told you that you are better than them because you were not a drug addict? On The contrary, you are worse than him in some way because you have not yet passed the life school which they had the chance to pass through.

If before me stands a former addict, it means that they can teach me how I can teach my children so that they do not embark on this path. If before me stands a man who doesn't know what it means to be a woman neither understands what price she pays daily, what she goes through daily because she is not a man. If before me stands a woman, it means that she can share with me what it is to be a woman, daily. If a woman has given birth to a child, even one, is that not enough reason to respect and honor her? If a beautiful woman stands before me, it is also an opportunity for me to honor her, to learn what she does to look so attractive. This is worthy of compliments! If a person older than me stands before me, it is already enough reason to honor them, because they have lived longer in this world than me, so without any question I honor them. Everyone deserves respect! That a man is older than me, allows me to see that at least in one thing he is already better than me, he has lived on this earth longer than me. If a woman is a mother and a wife, she is definitely better than me, because I never was a mother and a wife!

All that distinguishes a person, everything that others have and I do not, is a reason not to humiliate but to respect. Even if I see a homeless person I must understand that they already have an experience which I do not have. They have surpassed me in the matter of survival on the street, they are more experienced, they have already passed through something, which I have not passed through and experienced what to me, is unknown. Maybe it is even a very negative experience, they have been there, but I have not. The homeless people are worth listening to, we can learn how they became so, what mistakes were made, that made them homeless. This will help me not to repeat their way to avoid the pain and frustration that became their lot. So when I see a homeless person, I should say to myself: *«Perhaps this person has done something wrong in life, since they ended up on the street where they are today but I could have been in their place. Kudos to this person, although they lost all and ended on the street yet did not commit suicide! What would I have done if I were in their place? I do not know! therefore, for this reason, they are worthy of respect».*

Robert Kiyosaki, author, best known for his book «Rich Dad, Poor Dad», *rightly said, do not work on other people, work on your thoughts about other people».* It is not our prerogative to judge or condemn people we meet on the road of life. Our task is not to find what you can use to despise or to look down a person. We should have no time to waste time *«to work on another person».* Our primary responsibility is to work on our *thoughts about the other person, that* we can as quickly as possible discover what we can honor them for. This isn't always easy. This is where all our efforts should be directed at. [4]

To revere another, you have to be healthy inside you need to know that you are not worse than others, you

---

[4] *Prerogative, in a broad sense - preemptive right on any - any duty; exclusive right to any - any activity that a specific or official; exclusive right on - or what - any action; advantage that someone - or has over the other.*

are also good in something you have the power and ability to enrich someone, to provide help. However, we should not impose ourselves or our services on others, we should not say: *«I am better than you, for this reason, I have the right to teach you!»* No, a person living under the law of difference does not act like this! A person who sees the difference in others and knows how to appreciate them, always approaches other people from the perspective of What *can I offer them? What can I do to serve that person?».* When you see the benefits or success in any area of another person, it is a signal to what you can learn from the person.

No love without respect for a person

We are religious enough to hate each other but not religious enough to love each other.

- Jonathan Swift (1667 - 1745), satirist, essayist, philosopher

The words of Irish writer, satirist, public activist, philosopher, poet, tells us that our religion is often only enough to hate or neglect each other but it is not enough to show one another love and respect, most importantly, respect. However, our humanity and spiritual maturity is expressed by the latter. How can we respond to the infirmities and weaknesses of our neighbor? How can we look for and find in their faults, fragments of a precious person created in the image and likeness of God, which is reflected in their unique gifts and talents in their unique role and mission on Earth?

You do not require huge costs of mental and moral strength to not appreciate the difference in people - to neglect and reject the value of any human person, one doesn't need much intellectual capacity. However, to learn to love a person and receive them as they are with all their uniqueness and differences, we need to raise our moral and ethical level to the proper level, where we know that we live in our daily lives according to the law of difference.

WITHOUT HONOR IT IS IMPOSSIBLE TO SHOW REAL LOVE TO PEOPLE. Without love, we pervert the nicest things that we would like to be engaged in, in our lives. These are well - known quotes:

Duty without love makes a person irritable

Responsibility without love makes an inconsiderate person

Justice without love makes a person brutal

TRUTH without love makes a person a critic

Education without love makes one two-faced

Intelligence without love makes one tricky

Friendliness without love makes one hypocritical

Competence without love makes a man unyielding

Power without love makes a man a rapist

Honor without love makes one arrogant

Wealth without love makes a person greedy

Faith without love makes a person a fanatic

All these are faulty traits:

- *irritability*
- *presumptuousness*
- *brutality*
- *complaining*
- *two-facedness*
- *deception*
- *hypocrisy*
- *non-compliance*
- *violence*
- *haughtiness*
- *greed*
- *extremism*

These traits occur only for one reason: we do not have enough love and respect for people, to whom we would like to be:

- *faithful*
- *responsible*
- *fair*
- *truthful*
- *good mannered*
- *clever*
- *friendly*
- *competent*
- *possessing positions of power, honor, wealth and faith*

Well, it would be good to take stock of **the next chapter** of this book. If you dear reader, have no objection, then let's proceed.

1. One of the most important principles of the law of the difference is that we need to learn to appreciate every person, no matter how insignificant they may seem to us. The answer to the question of why? is very simple: God created each person unique, and therefore each person has an advantage over me - each person in one - area exceeds me. The understanding of this fact must be seriously rooted in our minds.

2. Of the first statement, we arrive at the second not less important conclusion: **We must look at every person as someone higher than us. As a student looks at the teacher, as if we are on our knees, in order to learn something very valuable from them to benefit us.** Indeed, it is this position of the heart that will help us to learn from this person and to accept what they have to enrich our lives. [5]

---

[5] *Postulate - approval, accepted without evidence and serve as the basis for the construction of a - a scientific theory.*

3. If we are presented with an alternative to see either the shortcomings or the dignity of people, for our own well-being it is better to choose the latter. This is the right focus for our view of the people around us. [6]

So, dear friends, we are done with our consideration of the second chapter of the book entitled the law of difference, which was devoted to studying the principles of this universal law. We found, how we are to look at each person, how we can learn to see the advantages of other people. We understood what we can honor people for and discovered that there is no love for a person without honor. In the next chapter, we will look at what it means to live under the law of difference. We will review the practical ways to show the expression of this law in our daily lives.

---

[6] *Alternative (fr. alternative, from Lat. Alternatus - the other) - one of the two or more mutually exclusive options, and each of these possibilities.*

GOLDEN TRUTH

The law of difference states that: everyone I see, every person on this earth was created by God and is unique, and everyone is in some way, better than me

To live by the law of difference, one must learn:

- *To see benefits other people*

- *notice the difference in other people*

If anyone can do something better than us or more than us, then the law of difference demands that we honor the person, whomever they may be

Our human nature pushes each of us to see people from the position of our personal advantages, we should see them better than we are and in a more favorable light

One of two things: either we look for shortcomings, or we seek dignity in others

Most people tend to notice the flaws of others

We must look at every human as someone who can enrich us

Only when we see difference, can we be enriched

All that distinguishes, all that others have, that I do not - is an occasion to honor and respect that person

We must appreciate what is in a person, even if we perceive he or she is worse than us

SELF – ASSESSMENT

1. How do you see other people?
1)I am the only and exclusive one (0)
2)There is someone better than me but I'm still better   than a lot of people (I do not sleep on the street, not begging, do not live on others) (1)
3)Each person on this earth has something better me (2)

2. Law of difference demands:
1)We can divide people into categories by their abilities and treat them according to a «Table of Ranks» (0)
2)That we be proud of the differences that we have (1)
3)That we recognize the dignity of a person, whoever he might be (2)

3. I look at the people around me and see:
1)Their disadvantages (0)
2)What I can help them (1)
3)What I can learn from them (2)

EVALUATION OF TEST RESULTS

(0 points) Unfortunately, the principles of the law of the differences are alien to your life. People for you are very unpleasant subjects who, in your opinion, spoil your life. It's hard for you to honor and respect people, because you cannot see, why they can be honored and respected. That's why you do not feel love for people and are not sure that they deserve your love. All is not lost! If you want to change your angle of view to learn how to love people through seeing their difference, further reading of this book with of all practical tasks at the end of each chapter will help you.

(1 - 5 points) Not bad! You are on the way to live in accordance with the law of difference and discern not only your own outstanding abilities, but also of other people near you. You realize that every person is worthy of respect from you but your actions do not always correspond to a person of the highest moral standard in your everyday life. Continue reading book and work on yourself with the help of the practical activities at the end of each chapter and your success is just around the corner!

(6 points) Congratulations! You have almost become a professional at noticing and discerning other people's difference. It seems that you have been immersed into the principles of the law of the difference since birth.

If so, thank your parents for being a well brought-up child because thanks to their efforts you do not have to suffer so much in life, as those who absolutely do not know about the existence of the law of difference.

Guidelines for the implementation of practical tasks

1. *CAUTION: These activities should not only be read and forgotten, they are VERY IMPORTANT. According to many years of working with people I know people often perform such tasks «for the sake of it" but it's your life, this is for you, take them seriously.*

2. *To maximize results, I suggest performing the tasks within the 24 hours, otherwise, you will forget, get distracted and you will distance yourself from the results you want.*

3. *To answer all the questions, find a quiet place and systematically work out the tasks.*

4. *Meditate on each chapter, on all the points that you underlined for yourself, reflect on the them and write out your steps of action.*

5. *Set yourself a time frame, constraints, to help you not to put off working on yourself.*

6. *Find someone you can be accountable to, who could help remind you to stay focused on working on yourself.*

Practical tasks

How should you look at each person you encounter in life? What position do you have to take in your heart towards people?

List the factors that allow us to respectfully treat other people. Please comment on each of them. How does this manifest in your life? What do you intend to do to change your present state of things?

Do you like people? How do the words of Jonathan Swift fit the description of your behavior in daily life: *«we are religious enough to hate each other but not religious enough to love each other»?* What do you think, what do you need to change in the way you relate to people? What are you going to do to get rid of the callousness and arrogance in your heart toward people who are weaker or what you deem «unworthy» of you?

Chapter 3

What does it mean to live by the law of difference?

What does it mean to live by the law of difference?

If we treat people how they deserve, they will remain the way they are, but if we relate to them as who they should and could be then they will become such.

- Johann Wolfgang von Goethe (1749 - 1832), poet, statesman, thinker

Well, dear reader, let's proceed to the next chapter of our narrative under the title «LAW OF DIFFERENCE». Let's recall that in the previous chapter we looked at this principle in all of its wonderful aspect. We have learned that people should not be looked down on, but rather with respect and reverence, discerning their advantages to find as quickly as possible what we could learn from them. We have in detail expanded on the reasons why every human-being must be honored. In this chapter, we will talk with about how to act according to the law of difference.

Johann Wolfgang von Goethe also tells something about this wonderful principle. I have used exactly his words as an epigraph to the second chapter of this book. German poet, statesman, thinker and scientist, Von Goethe offers us to treat people according to the way they "should and could be", because it promises us hope, that they those people will become how we expect them to be! The Path *«to deal with a person as he deserves»* Von Goethe admitted leads to a dead-end because in the end at the person would remain as he was, this means nothing new awaits us if we tread this path.

Though I must confess honestly, that it is sometimes risky to relate to people on a credit of high trust without first giving them time to prove their worth: he has not yet earned a good relationship from your side, and you seem to risk being deceived in your expectations. The risk? Sure! But this risk promises us great dividends in the future. By acting exactly this way, we can expect positive changes in people, that we so much want to see in them. So, do not get stuck in your past fears and insecurities and worries, do not cling to something that reminds you of your bitter experience. Thinking like this: *«all people are the same! They were, they are, and will be the most malicious creatures in the world! People do not change, so DO NOT trust them, they will deceive you, betray and cast you out!»*. To think like this is the *most* harmful activity in the world. Open your heart for a new turn in your life - it's not as bad as it may seem at times! It is worth learning and trying to trust people in order to taste life at its best, it is worth believing the best in people, so that one day they will pleasantly surprise us. I want to make the following statement: **to enjoy the uniqueness of people around us, and to live by the law of differences, we need to:**

- see God in people

- know that every person is worthy of respect even for
- the sake of Him who created them

- notice the advantages of people

- see good qualities in people

- compliment people

- honor and esteem people highly

- rejoice in their successes

- praise people, say something good about them

- notice each person's unique value, despite their shortcomings

- realize that each person has something - something special

- see in every person something good and pleasant

- respect a person for their genuine value

- note in the person their uniqueness

Observe people!

One family came to the restaurant for lunch. The waitress took the order from the adults and then turned to their seven-year-old son.

- What do you want to order?

The boy timidly looked at the adults and said:

- I'd like a hot dog.

No sooner had the waitress written the order, that the mother intervened:

- No hot dog! Bring him a steak with mashed potatoes and carrots.

The waitress ignored her words.

- You want hot dog with mustard or ketchup? She asked the boy.

- With ketchup.

- I'll be there in a minute, waitress said, and went into the kitchen.

At the table deafening silence reigned. Finally, the boy looked at the audience and said:

- know what? She thinks I'm real! [3]

Do you find it pleasant when people notice you when you walk into a room? Would you like people see you as nothing or pay attention to you? Welcome and treat you as a respected person or ignore you? Just as it was pleasant to the little boy in the story above, in the same way everybody wants to be treated as a HUMAN BEING - valued, appreciated, noticed, not passed by or ignored as if he's not there. Can we do this in our daily lives? If so, then honor people, you see!

I have a tradition: I do not pass by people without paying them any attention! If I walk past someone either I make sure I smile, or say "Hi!" or with the aid of gestures make the person understand that I see them. I notice EVERYBODY! I behave the same on the street, where people are not familiar with me. Even though I don't know them, I continue to notice them. **Become such people!**

Begin to notice people! After all, people are not a wall, not a forest, not the trees, people are not furniture or figurines. Observe each person! Celebrate the clothes in which they are dressed in, the color of the clothes, hairstyle, lipstick, make-up, how beautiful they are. Or note those who needs your help: maybe a person is not so beautiful, this should be the more reason why they need your attention because they may lack something. Think about who you can help or advise.

Be interested in people!

In each person lies something precious,
which no one else has.

- Israel Baal Shem Tov (1698 - 1760), founder of the
Hasidic movement in Judaism

People have a need that interest be demonstrated towards them but we are so busy with their own affairs that we ignore people. We need to remember that everyone is gifted in some field, everyone has a talent. **If your life revolves only around yourself it is a meager and very poor life.** Once in the company of people, I always find at least five people, to whom I want to go near and communicate with. I can discover and see in these people what is not in me, I am sure that the dialogue with them will enrich me. I mean each of us, each one of us is a multi-faceted personality, and through dialogue with a specific person I can discover a new word, a new quality, a new style, make a new discovery. I also know that the gift of a person can enrich me through communication because it becomes mine also.

I'm sure many of us have read the biography of great men: Theodore Roosevelt, Martin Luther King Jr., Abraham Lincoln, Frederick Douglass. All these people lived in the old days. Those who are our contemporaries, perhaps they are not Lincoln or King Jr. but each one is unique and have their own characteristics, which we can discover through communication.

We need to be interested in people to see what we can learn from them. The most important part of my study is based on what I see and hear. Therefore, I am interested in people, I know that everyone knows something I don't know, everyone has some wealth that is unknown to me, and I need to discover it for myself. I am interested in people first, to see the good in them, to see the uniqueness in them, through which I could learn valuable and useful lessons. Without exaggeration I can say that I AM LEARNING FROM EVERYBODY, this is my first task, my first question, when I see before me a new person: what can I learn from them? *This is my life attitude. I am sincerely interested in people. Can you say the same about yourself?*

Every person should be regarded as a Klondike, as wealth, as a huge deposit of precious materials. I consider every conversation as an opportunity to reveal another source, another wealth. Only then I start thinking: how can I enrich this person? How do I help them? Who can I introduce to them to, to achieve even greater success? To whom can I tell their story? What can I offer this person? In what direction can I help them develop? etc.[7]

---

[7] *Klondike - a region in the north - western Canada, east of the border with Alaska. Klondike became infamous - for the gold rush that began in 1897 - m and ending in the next year. Later the word «Klondike» has become synonymous, and came to mean a place full of countless treasures.*

Start getting interested in people! Usually we are too proud, arrogant and full of ourselves to go to other people and show sincere interest in them. To be interested in human beings, we need to be humble. We need to break our ego, our pride, to overcome our indifference and talk with people. When we are interested in a person, this is primarily an opportunity for us to practice humility. After all, to see the good, the uniqueness and positive in another person, it is necessary to come down from the high horse and humble oneself, in order to see the benefit in another person. *We must become truly free, to be interested people!*

I want to tell you the following methods that can help you implement being interested in people:

- *approach people*
- *acquaint yourself with them*
- *talk about who you are*
- *ask questions:*

  - *«what are you doing?»*

  - *«where are you from?»*

  - *«you look like a business lady, you do business?»*

  - *«you look like a TV Star. do you work on television?»*

- *«Wow, you have a great hairstyle, did you do it yourself or a hair stylist worked on you?»*

- *«you have a beautiful make-up. can you teach me how you do it?»*

- *«I like the way you look. can you tell me about yourself?»*

- *«You're a very interesting person, you attract people to you»*

- *« you have the most beautiful eyes I ever saw»*

- *«Hello! You have such an interesting look, do you by chance do advertising?»*

- *«you are a very elderly person and you still do self - development, why are doing this?»*

- *«you have such an original hair style do you follow fashion?»*

- *«Are you a student? What are you studying?»*

- *«are you an athlete? How do you manage to stay in shape?»*

- *«are you a businessman? You look very professional...»*

With these questions, I try to «pull» from any person, words to start a conversation and get to know more about them. Make sure that people around you feel needed!

MAKE COMPLIMENTS!

You cannot imagine the scroll with compliments which every artist carries along: a gentle friendly tap on someone's shoulder, newspaper clippings, words of encouragements spoken by a teacher, probably so - called faith in oneself is the foundation of our talent, but I'm sure that these encouragements are the cement with which our foundations are strengthened.

- Luciano Pavarotti (1935 - 2007), Italian opera singer

Encouragements, compliments bring not only pleasure to the artist; everyone keeps in their heart all the kind words that have been said about them, all the different demonstrations of sympathy and friendship towards them: friendly taps on the shoulder, warm handshakes, a word of encouragement or comfort. A person in this way blooms and performs at his or her best, showing their best qualities just as the flower stretches toward sunlight. We all long for those "verbal hugs" to keep us doing our best.

A lot of people don't know that they are special, so they live in negative emotions and have low self - esteem. People try to hide their problems behind clothes, make-up, hairstyles, accessories and so on. The truth is COMPLIMENTS HAVE AWESOME POWER, just one compliment can:

- *greatly enhance human psyche*

- *help people, even for a moment, forget about their problems*

- *restore people and their dignity*

- *to help people to see the positive side*

- *provide the chance for people to find themselves in life*

RECOGNIZING THE UNIQUENESS OF A PERSON CAN CHANGE HIS DESTINY! John Kehoe in his book, «THE CONSCIOUSNESS CAN DO ALL THINGS» describes how important, no matter what, to see in everyone, even the one who presents no hope for positive change, their values and unique difference; which you can do by thanking the person and giving encouragement and compliments.

John made a trip to the United States with his friend and his family, lecturing. They were forced to quickly hire a baby sitter, who happened to be one of the most negative people that they had ever known, the woman was always dissatisfied with everything. Of Course, this repelled people around her, no one wanted to have anything to do with her. John too, was put off by her.

Realizing what was happening and that something was wrong, he decided to change his approach to this woman. Logically he imagined that somewhere in the depths of her soul, she is a sensitive, sweet and cheerful person. Then he focused on this thought, drawing a new image of the woman. He imagined her like this a long while until these thoughts about her formed a smile on his face, as a ray of light that appeared in his life.

Once again, when the babysitter came, John took the woman aside and told her: «you know, every time, when you enter the house, It seemed to me like a ray of light just came in the reaction of the woman was predictable: she looked at him dumbfounded. John continued, «we very much appreciate you and that you are working as a babysitter for us, we are very happy that we have such a person as you. The woman smiled for the first time and when the others came out of the room, she said to him, «You know, nobody ever said such nice words as you just did to me. Never, Never, in my whole life.»

From that moment on, John always praised this woman, and every time she appeared, he would say, look! here comes our ray of light! With time, the woman changed radically. She stopped complaining about everything, became very nice and amazingly, the wrinkles on her face vanished, and the woman began to look twenty years younger. She really turned into a ray of light. [4]

We absolutely can break the ice of mistrust in human hearts with our kind words. We can become those agents of positive change that the whole world is waiting for! I think that we still underestimate the power that is contained in compliments. If we understand this and begin to release this positive energy into people in which we discern difference, even if potentially, wonders await us. People will be surprised at how nice and good they can be, if they decide to see people exactly like this.

Consciously look for the positive in people

Often people think to show –off by pointing out the flaws in people but this really shows their own weakness. The nicer and kinder people are the more they see the good in people, and the more foolish and meaner they are, the more they see the flaws in others.

- H. N. Tolstoy (1828 - 1910), Russian writer, thinker

WE SHOULD KNOWINGLY FOCUS ON THE POSITIVE, THAT IS IN A PERSON, NOT THE NEGATIVE. This claim is very well illustrated by the following parable.

One wise man gathered his disciples and showed them a clean sheet of paper in the middle of which was a fat black dot, asked:

— what do you see?

- a Point! - said one of the students who raised his hand first.

- Black dots - decided to clarify the other.

- Bold black dot - summed up the third.

— and what do you still see here? - decided the wise man to make his question more concrete but no could add anything. Then the wise man, frustrated, bowed his head down and wept.

- Tell us, why are you crying so bitterly? —asked the disciples surprised.

- I cried because all my disciples saw only a black dot, and no one noticed a large white sheet, said the sage.

How often do we just judge people only by their small, albeit noticeable shortcoming, ignoring and forgetting about their virtues!

It is not wise to focus on one small dot, when all of the remaining space is a pure white sheet of paper. It is not wise, intently, as if through a magnifying glass, to consider a small black dot and at the same time lose sight of and neglect, all the riches of the pure space that, is just next door. This attitude makes us to be bias, we choose to carefully and meticulously study one aspect of the paper and ignore and refuse to take notice of the remaining part of the paper which is relatively larger?

We must remember: THAT NO PERSON CAN BE COMPLETELY PERFECT. If we would examine each person we would find good and bad. Each person was originally created good by God. If they have anything bad in them, it is only because the evil of this world, ups and downs of life, crippled them and distorted the original image printed in him by the Creator. In every person there is something positive, no person can be only evil. Even if a person has 99% from 100% negative traits, you must diligently seek and find the positive in them, that 1% positive that should be emphasized through compliments. If they have 99% negative traits, it will not be easy to find the positive traits, because the negative will cry out for our attention, while the positive in the person will be hidden somewhere deep inside. By searching for the positive, we build people, not destroy them. French actress Juliette Binoche (b. in 1964) said words of great power: *«the strong is not the one who can knock down his opponent with a glance but the one who is able to raise up another from his knees with a smile!»* We must be people who raise others up from their knees, encourage, motivate and inspire them to become better than they were before they met us. Their disadvantages, should not be used as an excuse why we knock them down to the ground.

When we will receive a person as a value, as God's creation from the beginning, then we can see through the weeds of their bad deeds, their glorious qualities, which are hidden, just like a treasure. In our life, to produce good is a lot harder than to produce mischief. You do not require a huge effort to grow weeds, weeds grow on their own, just stop cultivating the piece of land in your possession and the weeds will take over. However, to grow wheat and convert it into bread, that is fit for food, a lot of effort is needed. By itself, grain cannot grow, it requires watering, care and cultivation. One weed can suppress valuable crops, if we will not try to prevent that from happening.

That is why we must invest a lot of effort, despite the evil, seek the good, so the negative does not blind us and we lose the ability to see the good and value that a person has. It takes more effort to awaken the human heart for goodness and light, while on the other hand to teach a person to do evil is not necessary, it seems to happen involuntary and naturally all by itself. Must human weaknesses make us to reject fellowship with an imperfect person? force us to delete them out of our lives? throw him into the trash where we dump useless things? Should the «thorns» cause us to give up the roses? Let's read the following story.

The Parable of the Rose

Once a man planted a rose, diligently took care of it, watered it and before it blossomed, he examined it. He saw a bud that should soon open up, he noticed the spikes on the stalk, and thought, «How can, from a plant with lots of prickly spikes grow a beautiful flower?» Saddened by this thought, he stopped to water the roses and the flowers died just before they blossomed.

This parable tells us that in every human soul there is a rose. All the divine qualities are potentially present in us at birth and they grow along with us, despite the thorns of our mistakes. Most people look at themselves and others and notice only those spikes, defects, shortcomings, failures, weaknesses. This leads people to despair, as they start to think that nothing good can come from those thorny stems. One of the great advantages which a person can have is the ability to accept their thorns and the thorns of others and find out no matter what is their rose. Only love can act this way: look at a person and being aware of their mistakes, not banish them from your life, but rather see and continue to appreciate the good in their heart.

Leo Tolstoy, revered as one of the greatest writers of the world, made a marked observation: *«Most people think to show off by pointing to the flaws of other people... »* that is, some people consider it an honor, their job, to discover the flaws of others, this however, is the easiest thing to do, it does not require much intelligence or strength. As the writer said, such people in this way, *".... only show their weakness.»*. There is no glory in engaging in such an occupation, it should rather serve as a negative signal because the more, *«... dumber and meaner, a person, the more he sees the flaws in others»*. On the contrary, the *«smarter and kinder a person, the more he sees the good in people.»*. What kind of person do you want to be among dear reader?

What makes us see negatives in others?

Only Fools notice mistakes in people and do not pay attention to their dignity. They are like flies that strive to sit only on the inflamed part of the body.

- Abu Al Faraj Ibn Haroun (1226 - 1286), the Syriac church leader, writer and scientist - encyclopedist

Allow me, dear reader, to present you:

The parable of the Seeker

A wise old man took a boy to the zoo.

- You see these monkeys?

- Yeah.

- Do you see the one that is running about seeking out fleas from the other monkeys?

— Yes.

- This monkey is a «seeker»! It believes others are infected with fleas and is trying to rid the other monkeys of the fleas.

— and the others, what?

- Nothing, just sometimes itchy.

- And who cleans «seekers»?

— No one. Therefore, he is the one with the most lice, most infected.

The tendency to notice only flaws is not a good trait. Especially when we seek the disadvantages of others. The way we look at people betrays, trying to hide behind the fine words and polite smiles. Constantly seeking the plusses and minuses of other people, we really show that we believe all around us are flea-infected flocks that urgently need to be «cleansed» of their shortcomings and disadvantages. Forgetting that the wise and observant eyes quickly determine who «the one with the most lice» in the zoo is. It is better to restrain your zeal in searching for the mistakes and drawbacks of others. If you have nowhere to put your time and energy, it is better directed in searching and fixing your own shortcomings.

The first thing that makes us see disadvantages in others is the desire to compete, to surpass, the desire to win over someone in something and as usual, at any price. Reasonable competition mobilizes our human strength and ability but when our sole purpose becomes 'destroying the enemy' to celebrate own victory, then we often slip into such a level of relationship where both sides will be losers.

Competition is characterized by state of visible or hidden competition for power, love, prestige, recognition, material prosperity, self - fulfillment but this state has the wrong motives and is destructive because of its very nature.

Soviet and Russian writer - fiction, literary critic and translator Alexander Mirrer (1927 - 2001) very aptly observed: *«Only slaves tend to feel joy at another's fall. The transition from servility to malevolence, that is the true mark of a slave.»* Often it results such consequences: one becomes a slave internally, sees disadvantages in others and feels joy because someone stumbled and fell, this is the true face of a slave. There is no need to spoil and distort your inner being and fall to such a low level.

Second thing is, we see disadvantages in others because of personal feeling of inferiority, because we do not believe in our self, we do not see our merits. When a person has complexes and low self-esteem, they think by raising another, they are putting themselves down. Things are not like this in the real sense, everything looks exactly the opposite: in raising another, we are growing in our eyes and in the eyes of others. **Only the «little» people tend to ignore others.** ONLY GREAT PEOPLE CAN SEE GREAT THINGS IN OTHERS.

To see negative is easy, we want to hide our own failure. Also, we are not ready to grow up to deal with our own faults. To analyze what is good in others, we do not want to strain or work hard to do. When we first notice the shortcomings in people, it only shows that we are not at peace with ourselves. We feel bad about ourselves, we suffer from some inner pain, and so we want to, belittle, look down on, count as nothing the dignity of others. We do not want to give the deserved honor to those who deserve it, we find it hard to express recognition, awe, reverence towards the other people, we do not want to commemorate, appreciate, celebrate the successes of others.

There is a saying by an unknown author that can be found on the internet: «*When a person does hurt us, most of the time, he is himself deeply unhappy. Happy people are not rude, do not swear in public transport, do not gossip about colleagues. Happy people live in a different reality. For them, all the above does not make any sense*». It is an amazingly beautiful illustration of the reality that is hidden in our daily routine. When we become witnesses to how people focus on the flaws of others tend to see in the first place disadvantages rather than advantages, we should be clear on why this is happening. It does not come from the fact that a person is happy, at peace or in state of inner peace. Rather, this behavior indicates that deep inside that person a problem has taken deep root and that person needs help.

Often, we see the negative in people because we envy them, also we are impatient, we do not want to learn, do not want to receive other people's wisdom about how they became more successful than us. The other reason is our pride, also that we are full of fear: «*what if this person can hurt me in some way?»* **The weightiest reason why we see the negatives first in people is our own self-centeredness, our own egocentrism, which is at the roots of all unhappiness in life.** If a person is currently focused on them self, if they are so self-absorbed that they live only for their problems, then sooner or later this will lead to depression.

Haroun, Syrian Christian activist, writer, scientist and encyclopedist concluded that only the foolish focus on the shortcomings of people, *«… and do not pay attention to their dignity. »* The foolishness of man forces him to ignore the positive in the others and with zeal and delight seek to find the negative. The Rotten inside of people makes them like *«flies that strive to sit only on the inflamed part of the body»*, with a *magnifying* glass in his hand to discover the slightest wormhole that can be found in humans. In addition, these people cause others discomfort and inconvenience that only an annoying insect can deliver. Therefore, the tendency to notice at first flaws and disadvantages in others only show the stupidity and morbid craving for festering wounds on the body of another person.

The importance to turn the focus from the shortcomings of others to oneself is well said by former Soviet and Russian poet, singer, novelist and screenwriter, songwriter Bulat Okudzhava Shalvovich (1924 - 1997):

Condemn first yourself,
Learn this kind of art,
And after Judge your enemy
And neighbors on the earth.

Learn first yourself

To not forgive a single blunders,
And after shout at your enemy,
That he is an enemy grievous are his sins.

Not in the other, but defeat the enemy in you,
And when you will succeed in this,
you no longer have to play the fool -
So you become a person.

Personally, I always think of a person only the best and in a positive way. Even if someone has a surplus of negatives, I always try to find understanding and explanation for their faults. It helps me to avoid a negative perception of the person. I do not understand how you can, thinking about others, remember only the negative thing. Just take into consideration that every person has so much wealth, so many interesting sides, so much energy, so much life, that to concentrate and remember about them only the worst, must take a lot of efforts! In my opinion, you should never think negatively about people!

What we look for, is what we find

If you can see the beauty, it is only because you carry beauty on the inside.

- Paulo Coelho (b. in 1947),
Brazilian writer and poet

It is no secret that we find in people WHAT WE STRIVE TO FIND. Most often our expectations, which we initially have in relation to a person are fulfilled. In connection with this idea, is a very interesting study that confirms my thought.

*The researchers enlisted the help of a group of school teachers. The school teachers were told that the choice fell on them because of their **exceptional** teaching abilities. In addition, they were told only gifted children will be admitted into their classes, but neither the children nor their parents will not know anything about this experiment because its goal is to see how gifted children will behave if they do not know about their abilities.*

As expected, the teachers wrote reports that children are doing exceptionally well. They also wrote, that work with these children – was a pleasure and that they would like to work with them continuously.

*In this project was one **secret addition**. Teachers did not know that they chose the students not based their exceptional abilities rather selection was made arbitrarily. In addition, children were not elected based on giftedness but chosen at random. But as expectations were high, the results were high. Since teachers considered themselves and the children exceptional they were able to achieve exceptional success.*

What does this mean for us? That our **predefined prejudices (expectations),** based on one or another information have strong influence on the way we listen to people, and what we ultimately hear. *If we can get rid of our prejudices or minimize them, then can we learn to really listen and hear each of those around us.* **Our bias can play a bad joke on us.** IF WE IN ADVANCE «WRITE OFF» A PERSON, THERE WILL NEVER BE ANYTHING IMPORTANT IN ANYTHING THEY WILL TRY TO SAY. If we listen carefully to each person as if their words are something important and something precious is hidden in them, it will happen in reality.

I would like to bring another fact in favor of my statement: **what we're looking for, is what we find.** In 1974, Langer and Abelson researchers carried out an experiment which showed the following. A Professional Psychology film was shown, in which the ordinary man answered a series of questions he was proposed. Psychologists were divided into two groups. The first group was told that they were witnessing the action of psychiatric patients, so it was not surprising that observing the patient, they concluded, that the man was not normal and showed signs of a bad adaptation. [5]

Psychologists should be independent experts, completely objective, however, they became influenced by the one who put them on this trial. Even they lost their sense of being objective: they became programmed by the opinion they were given concerning the man and became partial while observing a normal person. The second group of subjects was told that this an ordinary person who is being interviewed for a job. Psychologists from this group found this man to be quite normal, and well-adapted. Notice how much our beliefs are influenced by the opinion of people we humans consider authoritative to us. We must take this into account when faced with the task of forming our own original and first-hand opinion about a person.

The Power of the impact which an authoritative opinion and the opinion of the majority can have on us is well conveyed in the documentary film, "I and Others" by director Felix Sobolev, filmed in 1971 at the studio Kievnauchfilm. The film consists of a series of social-psychological experiments that paint a vivid picture of how much we are really NOT independent in our judgments. One of the most interesting experiments is called «A scientist or a criminal?»

In the experiment, the hall in turns invited subjects, each of which demonstrated a portrait of the same man.

Then each of the participants was asked to describe the man who was depicted in the portrait, to describe how they saw him. The most interesting is that initially one group of participants was told that the portrait is that of a criminal and others that the portrait is that of a scientist. Those participants who had previous knowledge of the portrait been that of a scientist, eagerly recognized the face of man, kind, gentle, and loving. Other participants based on their initial knowledge the portrait was that of a criminal, immediately saw in his outline clear signs of cruelty, treachery and baseness. [6]

If the participants had not been previously given any explanations, then they would not have found it so hard to give an unbiased opinion. But because each of them initially heard an authoritative opinion, it appeared that developing an independent judgment of the person they had seen in the portrait, was not easy. The participants easily found facts to support the initially presented opinion about what they were seeing. They used their imaginations, writing variations on the given theme they started «seeing» something that was not there and stopped seeing what was obvious. That is, they found it easy to find that, which with the help of the initial clue given by the moderator, was to be found.

It would probably be interesting for you to know, dear reader, that the creation of this documentary, "I and Others", was motivated by the experiments of Solomon Eliot Asch the results of which were published in 1951. The aim of these experiments was to demonstrate the power of conformity in groups. Studies of Solomon Asch found that subjects joined the majority opinion in 37% of cases. The subject refused to believe what he saw *with his own eyes* and yielded to the pressure of the group, thereby demonstrating its conformity. [7] But we cannot afford to become conformists viewing and assessing other people. [8]

If I do not get the right information about a person, almost automatically I get a negative information about him, and the negative destroys not only the person, but also me. For me it's not enough that someone tells me something about someone. I do not want to believe what I am told, I want to get accurate information firsthand from the person. That's why I'm looking for a way to allow everyone to speak, to listen to everyone, hear the story of the lives of everyone who I meet along the way. For me, it is important to get objective information, based not only on labels that can arise because their physical appearance, behavior or perception of others. Do not be satisfied only by what you can see with your physical eyes. *If we do not live like this, it means that we live in speculation, we place yokes on people, hang labels on them.* If we do not form our own views about people by talking to them and getting to know them, it means that we live on the basis of false information. I always need truthful information so that I do not live in the negative, and under the weight of prejudice and bias.

---

[8] *Conformity (from pozdnelat. Conformis - « like «,») - склонность сообраз-ный » their attitudes, IHQ's, and according to opinions, that prevails in the community.*

Be friendly!

Pauline and Vic were friends. They had been friends since high school, and now they had a lot in common, for example, dancing classes in the evenings three times a week. One time Pauline took offense against Vic and said in heart to her: «You're not interested in my life! do not even sympathize! You are not interested in what with happens to me! »

Vic did not understand what was happening. It turns out that Pauline was responding to what happened between them the other day. The girls had agreed to go together for rehearsals but Pauline suddenly said: «I am sick, I feel bad, I cannot go anywhere», and Vic did not find anything better to say as: « Well, since you feel bad, I will go alone, but you should rest!»

But it turns out that Pauline needed something else: which was that she not only be left alone but that someone support her, play an active role in her life, by asking, «what happened? how do you feel». Pauline wanted her best friend to suggest: «Let me pick you up and we'll go together!» It turns out, exactly this was what Pauline needed but Vic did not understand this and Pauline became offended decided that their communication had become too formal.

If our best friends act like this, then what can we say about the people on the street! Often, we are not able to show sincere interest, even in relation to our loved ones. We do not notice, we remain deaf and blind to what is happening to them even though we could be living with the person.

one day a sage was asked:

- How many types of friendship are there?

- Four, - he said. - There are friends like food - every day you need them.

There are friends like medicine - you look for when you feel bad.

There are friends like disease - they are looking for you.

But there are friends who are like the air - they are not visible but are always with you.

As we can see, friendship can be different. There are friends that we need every day. There are friends, we look for only when we feel bad. There are friends that are looking for us and there are those who remain with us always, under any circumstances, no matter what happens. Sometimes they are invisible, like air, but *sometimes*......that's exactly what we really need.

How do real friends behave? Let the following parable be an illustration of the kind of friendship people around us expect from us:

On a field, two horses are grazing. From afar it seems that they are common and unremarkable horses. If you came closer, you would probably notice something that is unusual. The eye one of them was blind. The Owner has not led her to the slaughterhouse but has cared for her and that alone was amazing.

After waiting a little bit listening, you would hear the sound of the bell. The bell was attached to the bridle of the second horse. The old horse heard its tinkling and always knew where her «tribeswoman» was and went behind her. If you had stopped and watched these two, you would have noticed how the young horse watched after the old, not going far so that the old horse could hear the bell and follow her. Coming back from the pasture, she occasionally stops, looks back, checking whether her friend is behind her.

Likewise, as the owner of these horses, the Creator does not give up on us because we are not perfect, or because we have a problem. He continues to be with us and sends us other people who help us when we need it. Often, we, like the blind horse survive, only thanks to someone or something God has brought into our lives, like soft tinkling of the bell, shows us the way. Also for us is prepared another role: we must become those, in whose hands whom God puts the bell so that we can lead others, helping them in puts the bell so that we can lead others, helping them in the difficult times of their lives. This is the meaning of friendship.

Do not take people for granted!

To all that is given to us in life, including communication and relationships with people, you can get used to them and this is dangerous. The danger is that you stop valuing that which you get used to, then you start taking it for granted and relate to it as common and as a result lose all respect and love for it. *Familiarity breeds contempt.* To be able to value each person according to the law of difference and not lose the dividends which relationship with them can provide, continue to keep a respectful and reverential attitude, it is important to:

avoid:

addiction

familiarity

continue to appreciate what we have.

In a Christmas letter to his nine-year-old daughter in 1966, investment analytic Harry Browne tried to explain to his daughter, that nothing in this world like love, kindness, respect from others should be taken for granted, you must receive it with due appreciation. He began his message to his daughter with the following lines.

Sweetheart, nobody owes you,

It's Christmas, and I have a common problem - what gift to choose for you. I know that you like books, games, clothes. However, I'm very selfish, I want to give you something - something that will stay with you longer than a few days or even years. I want to give you something that will remind you of me every Christmas. You know, I think I chose the gift already: I'll give you one truth that took me a lot of years to absorb. If you understand it now, you will enrich your life in hundreds of different of ways and it will protect you from trouble in the future.

So here it is: nobody owes you,

This means that no one is living for you, my child. Because no one is you. Everybody lives for them self. The only thing a person can feel — is their own happiness. IF YOU WOULD ONLY UNDERSTAND THAT NO ONE SHOULD ORGANIZE YOUR HAPPINESS, YOU WILL BE FREED FROM THE EXPECTATION OF THE IMPOSSIBLE.

This means that no one is obliged to love you. If someone does love you it means you possess something special that makes them happy. Find out what it is and try to make it stronger and then, you will be loved even more.

When people do something for you, this is only because they wanted to do it. Because you have something in you - something so important to them, that it stirs up a desire in them to do what will make you like them. It is not because they owe you. If your friends want to be with you, this is not out of a sense of duty.

No one should respect you, *and some people will not be kind to you. At that moment, when you learn that no one is obliged to do you and that some may be unkind to you, you will learn to avoid such people because even you do not owe them anything.*

Again: nobody owes you.

You must be an Ace, the best, for you first. *If you make it, other people will want to be with you, want to give you different things in exchange for what you can give them and some people will not want to be with you and the reasons might not be in you. If that happens - just look for other relationships. Do not let someone else's problem become yours.*

In the moment when you realize that the love and respect of others must be earned, you will not be waiting

waiting for the impossible, and you will not be disappointed. Others do not have to share their properties, thoughts or feelings. And if they do, it is only because you earned it and then you can be proud of the love that you deserve, and sincere respect of friends. Never take it all for granted. If you do - you will lose all these people. They are not «yours by right», to seek them and «earn» them, must be your daily pursuit.

It was like a mountain had fallen from my shoulders, when I realized that no one owes me. While I thought that everybody owed me, I spent an awful lot of, physical and emotional, energy to get what I wanted. In fact, no one owes me good behavior, respect, friendship, politeness, or their intellectual capacity. At the time when I understood this, I started getting a lot of satisfaction from all my relationships. I focused on the people who wanted to do the things that I needed from them and it's served me well - with friends, business partners, lovers, customers and strangers. I always remember, that I can get what I want, only if I enter into a peaceful agreement with the person I am interacting with. I must know how he thinks, what is important to him, what he eventually wants. Only under these conditions can I get what I really expect. Only after I have taken time to understand a person, can I know if I really need something from him. Not so easy to sum up in one letter that which took me many years to understand. Maybe, if you would re-read this letter every Christmas, it would make sense for you every year a little bit more clearly. NOBODY OWES YOU.

When we begin to understand one simple truth that no one owes us, it becomes easier to live. We then cease to relate to people from a selfish point of view looking for what we can gain from communicating with them. We cease to assess a person in terms of usefulness for ourselves and begin to pay attention to what we can give through our relationship with them.

We begin to appreciate all the good that comes from this person in our lives. We beginning to see them as a jewel and this stirs in us reciprocal feelings of gratitude. We begin to see the other person as a unique personality, a person with unique and exclusive features and it allows us to raise them to a place of esteem. With this attitude towards them as somebody very special, it becomes easier for us to reverence and recognize the dignity of the person. So, we begin to live according to the law of difference every day of our lives. That makes our lives easier, more beautiful and more fulfilled. Thus, we are increasing the number of good, allowing its light to illuminate more and more people.

So, we will draw conclusions on this third chapter of the book « Law of Difference »

1. To live in obedience to the law of difference, is simple. If you:

- *notice people*

- are interested in people

- compliment people

- consciously look for the positive in people

- be faithful friends

- do not take people for granted, you will not find it difficult to live in harmony with others.

2.**Our life should not revolve around us.** If so, it is a wasted life.

3.**A kind word can revive the human soul, and radically change his fate.** When we speak positive words to a person, we exalt him in such a way to the level to which we have informed him, through our positive words. The person will be forced to stretch them self to the standard that we have set through our spoken word.

So, we have come to the end of another chapter of the book «The Law of Difference«. In it, we considered how to live by the law of difference, in practice by applying its principles and provisions. In the next chapter, we will turn our attention directly to what the law of difference says and what it claims. We'll see, dear reader, what our natural response to the differences of others are.

It often looks like this:

- we seek friendship with those who are similar to us

- we reject those who are different from us

In this chapter we also learn, what we really need. Finally, we turn our attention to the fact that very often we begin to appreciate something only when we lose it. In order to not make similar errors, we strongly recommend you continue reading this book!

GOLDEN TRUTH

People - are not a wall, not a forest, not trees,

people - are not furniture, so you need to notice each person

People feel the need for others to be interested in them but we are so busy with our own affairs that we neglect people

It is not wise to focus on a black dot at a time when all the remaining space is a perfect white sheet of paper

We need to consciously focus our attention on all that is positive in a person, not on the negative

Nobody will be perfect

The weightiest reason why we see the shortcomings of people is our own self - centeredness, which is the basis of all unhappiness in life

We FIND in others, what we SEEK to find

It is necessary to avoid familiarity so we don't lose what we have

SELF - ASSESSMENT

1.When I walk past people...
　　1)I do not see them even at close range! (0)
　　2)Periodically, I am just so focused on myself that I just do not notice people (1)
　　3)With any available means I try to inform people that I am glad to see them (2)

2.Do you neglect the others?
　　1)Yes (0)
　　2)50/50 (1)
　　3)No (2)

3.How often do you compliment people?
　　1)Never (0)
　　2)Sometimes 1)
　　3)Constantly (2)

4.What do you usually notice about people?
　　1)I see something negative in them (0)
　　2)Periodically, I am so focused on myself that I just don't notice people (1)
　　3)I Make every effort to ensure that I consciously focus my attention on the positive (2)

5.Are you a person with a tendency for familiarity?
1)Yes (0)
2)Sometimes (1)
3)No (2)

6.Are you a good friend?
1)No (0)
2)Not always (1)
3)Yes (2)

EVALUATION OF TEST RESULTS:

(0 - 5 points) Unfortunately, you have a hard time living by the law of differences. Most likely, you do not even aspire to it. It seems nothing has inspired you to see something good or of great value and exciting in people. People around you in your imagination, are full of disadvantages and shortcomings. Even in a jar of honey you would find a dead fly, that is, any little thing is enough to blind you from all the many good qualities of a person. With this attitude to others, you risk becoming unsociable, fixed only on yourself and your problems. Such a life does not represent any pleasure. You risk your mental and emotional health, if you do not embark on radical changes in your life. You can fulfill them using this book: read it through and do all the tasks at the end of each chapter. Then you have the chance to enjoy the beauty of life and become a happier person and making others around you happy as well!

(6 - 11 points) Not bad! You are probably already practicing a good fraction of those tips, which you have had time to read in this chapter. You have a good chance to become a healthy and happy person! In all aspects, our life in general, depends on how harmonious our relationships with others are: life satisfaction, happiness, health and peace of mind. You have succeeded in noticing people and are interested in them, with varying success you compliment them, and this has even started to bring you pleasure and joy. You exert all effort to find the positive in others, and believe me, your efforts will sooner or later translate into success! This book you are holding in your hands will help you not to lose this optimistic attitude. Further reading this book will help you improve your skills of living by the law of difference every day of your life.

(12 points) Congratulations! Judging by the results, you are already doing well in the practice of the law of the difference in your life. Your wisdom will pay off handsomely, one hundred-fold! Only wisdom closes our eyes to the flaws of others and opens us to see and notice the dignity of people, turning a blind eye to their shortcomings. Only wisdom focuses us on the 1% of positive traits of a person rather than rejoice while watching 99% of his mistakes and errors. Your ability to appreciate people's dignity will lead you to a happy and fulfilling life in ALL aspects. Even now, don't forget to continue to share your skills and gifts with those around you, those you can help by serving them with your abilities. You can provide substantial assistance to these people.

GUIDELINES FOR THE IMPLEMENTATION OF PRACTICAL TASKS

1. *CAUTION: These activities should not only be read and forgotten, they are VERY IMPORTANT. According to many years of working with people I know people often perform such tasks «for the sake of it" but it's your life, this is for you, take them seriously.*

2. *To maximize results, I suggest performing the tasks within the 24 hours, otherwise, you will forget, get distracted and you will distance yourself from the results you want.*

3. *To answer all the questions, find a quiet place and systematically work out the tasks.*

4. *Meditate on each chapter, on all the points that you underlined for yourself, reflect on the them and write out your steps of action.*

5. *Set yourself a time frame, constraints, to help you not to put off working on yourself.*

6. *Find someone you can be accountable to, who could help remind you to stay focused on working on yourself.*

PRACTICAL TASKS

What do the words of Johann Wolfgang von Goethe tell you: *"if we treat a person as he deserves, he will remain as he is but if you treat him as a person he can and should be, he will become that person?"* What conclusions do you derive from this statement? How, in practice, will you apply the lessons from this quotation, from this principle?

What is your understanding of living by the law of difference? What methods and ways can you achieve this in your daily life? List and comment on the ways you are going to expand your skills in communicating with people.

Do you agree with the fact that recognizing the uniqueness of a person can change their destiny? Has something like this happened in your life? How are you going to practice this principle, how are you going to change the fate of people around you using this hint?

CHAPTER 4

WHAT THE LAW OF DIFFERENCE CLAIMS?

WHAT THE LAW OF DIFFERENCE CLAIMS?

Well, friends, we are about to start a new chapter of the book «The Law of Difference». To begin with, I want to ask you:

- Do you know about the Law of the difference?

- Do you live by it?

If you lived by the law of difference, you would have made complimenting people more and more your business, especially those of your own family, friends and relatives. Exactly to this end the previous chapter dedicated. In it I explained in detail, all the different ways that in practice will help you, dear reader, fulfill all your good intentions, how to notice and appreciate the difference of other people, those you meet every day of your life. In this chapter, we will look at the law itself and its claims. So, there is a law of difference that:

- gives the ability to see in what way one person differs from another

- helps to see difference between the purpose of one person and that of the other

- gives an insight into why it is necessary to reverence the uniqueness of others

- teaches you to cherish the people around you: to see their beauty, to understand that you also need other people

- causes you to humble yourself and reverence others: that which every husband and every wife should do in their family

The law difference is the ability to discern the differences in people, their gifts, potential and abilities. IF I SEE THE DIFFERENCE IN A PERSON, ONLY THEN CAN I GET SOMETHING OF VALUE FROM THEM! Not only can I do something valuable for them but they can also for me. If I do not see difference in a person then I can't get anything from them that could enrich me. If you do not see the difference in your wife, you will not appreciate her. **The law of difference helps to understand the difference between men and women, thus allowing us to understand and honor the role of each other.** Why do we fall in love? What makes us breathless? **WE ARE ATTRACTED BY WHAT WE LACK.**

The law of difference draws our attention to the uniqueness of each person and teaches us to appreciate it. Let us consider a classic example: when Adam saw Eve, he saw a difference in her. Adam noticed that her skin was different than his own: more delicate and smooth and pleasant to touch. Her hair was softer, she had flexible and graceful movements, she even thought and perceived the world around her differently, more emotionally. She was not as powerful physically: her height and build was different than that which Adam discovered in himself. He did not see in Eve, the developed muscles, which he was so proud of. The pitch of her voice was higher than his own, and on her face, was no vegetation, no facial hair. Eve had also a small waist, which visually emphasized more curved hips and broader breasts than that of Adam. Isn't that what attracted the first man to the woman? He saw that before him was an entirely different person.

Even though Eve looked, at first glance, like Adam, a human being with one head, two arms and legs, he could see that in her were some differences that attracted him to her. Moreover, he found that she was desirable for him. Thanks to the law of difference, Adam decided, it would not be profitable to neglect such a person, it might even be better to honor her because she was different in comparison to him. These differences, which Adam saw, made him to humble himself and respectfully esteem the other person, Eve his wife, above himself. I want to tell you that this is how every man must behave himself in his house and this is also what every wife should do in her house.

Why any man can fall in love? Because he saw the difference he saw that in this woman, was something he did not have. If you put Victor next to Andrew and Mary, whom will Victor choose? In whom is it more likely to fall

in love? To whom will Victor likely turn his attention: to the girl or the guy?

Normally man to man is not interesting because he is also a man, for this reason Andrew will not be able to compete fairly with Mary because he is the same as Victor so he is not interesting, not attractive to Victor. However, when Mary passed by Victor he was attracted to her, why? because there is a difference between them and the situation changes dramatically. She is attractive for him because there are differences between them. **WE ARE ATTRACTED BY THE THINGS THAT ARE DIFFERENT TO US.**

So, when people tell you that you are different, then it is the best compliment that can be. Your difference in comparison to others is the real you, and this is your uniqueness. Your uniqueness, your difference is what sets you apart from others and will give you value in the eyes of other people, you will be able to assist them in the area of your difference. **Never seek where you are similar to others!** Always seek to see what makes you different. Because you will only be able to enrich the surrounding people with that which differentiates you from them. When you are different, you can complement others in this: someone has lack in this area and you have a surplus and vise-versa. It is for this reason a man's attention is likely to be attracted by a woman, but not another man, because the other man is the same as him. *But a girl....* she is something special, she draws our attention!

It is a myth to think that we are attracted to that to which we are similar. We often say, "opposites attract" and there is good reason for that. It's a crazy idea or thought to say: "We are so similar that I want to spend the whole of my life with a person that's the same as I". THAT WHICH IS THE SAME AS YOU DOES NOT ENRICHES YOU. **Only what is different from you, can complement you.** Only someone who has something you do not, can you supplement. Only someone who has something you do not, you can strengthen. If you have something that the other has: mustache and beard, then with what can he strengthen you? Maybe, to give birth to your child? No! Therefore, when Andrew passes Victor, he does not pay any attention to him but when Mary passed by, she immediately attracted his attention. She caught his attention, not because she was the same as he, not because she has a mustache and a body structure like him. No, but because she is completely different: thin, beautiful, no mustache, but instead there are breasts, which he does not have and this her difference is what attracted his attention to her.

OUR NATURAL RESPONSE TO THE DIFFERENCES OF OTHER PEOPLE

We seek friendship with those who are similar to us
As a partner, you have to find someone who
complements your skills.

- Jack Ma (b. in 1964),
Founder of China's largest electronic
trading platform Alibaba

50-year-old entrepreneur Jack Ma argues that the best choice of a partner is someone who in the best possible way complements your skills. Jack Ma knows what he is saying. This is a man who for many years firmly holds a place on the list of the world's richest people with a fortune of $12 billion. A man who was able to organize such a business of world impact the Alibaba - (*Group*) with a capitalization of $230 billion surely, he does not need to relate with someone who is just like him, as two drops of water but those who as a result of the power and the wealth of their differences could compensate and therefore strengthen. [8]

Usually, we are looking for friendship with those who are similar, because we feel comfortable with people like us. Those who are different from us, are often rejected by us. If you want to take a leadership position in life and you find that people do not follow you, the reason may be that in you look for and choose only those with whom you are comfortable. Please understand: with those people you feel comfortable, you'll never grow because they will create a comfort zone for you. **Someone who is just like you, will never strengthen you and will neither be able to complement, nor enrich you.** The person who is the same as you, cannot enrich you. *You can be enriched only by those who are different from you.* Celebrate the differences of other people! Do not neglect differences. *Ignoring the differences of others, we deprive ourselves of the most valuable opportunity in life!* ONLY WHAT IS DIFFERENT FROM US, CAN STRENGTHEN US.

Do you know why we are drawn to and desire to be around those people whose character is the same as ours? Because with people, who are like you, you are comfortable, like-minded people do not challenge us, they allow us to relax, so you do not need to work hard to develop certain qualities. In doing so, you are cheating. CHEATING IN THE SENSE THAT SUCH A WAY OF LIFE LEADS TO POVERTY. **All of that allows a person to be lazy and leads to dishonor, destruction and degradation.** Have you not heard the news from Hollywood: the more successful, the more comfortable a person becomes in their life, the more they are drawn to drugs, alcohol, divorce, madness, anything comes into their lives! I want to confidently say: comfort is not useful to you, it will destroy your life, so it is not recommended for you! When you are drawn to the same person as you, which has your tendencies, similar inner desires, it will be harmful to you in the long run.

Do not be surprised that **God will always send your way those who would challenge you, those who are different from you.** You will be uncomfortable with people different from you but they are exactly those who will force you to change! If we remain in this state of comfort, it means we do not change, we remain the same, just as the stagnant swamp and because of this our life will give off a «stench», created by our faults and weaknesses. In the words of Simeon, an Athenian Monk, words that are still relevant even in our days: *«God has always surrounded us by people through whom we can be healed of our shortcomings.»* **Our life, is to some extent a path of healing eliminating those errors that have taken root in our character, behavior patterns, our relationship with people and so on.** Also, because we are imperfect, our way of life is partly destined to help us get rid of any kind of «filth» that darkens our existence.

Thanks to the people who are «working» on us, those that are not like us, they step on our favorite «wounds», persuading readjustment, we become better, stronger and more efficient. These people often irritate us, but thanks to them we change. Remember: exactly 'these kind of people' will come our way. **We do not need to look for people like us!**

Do not wait or expect people that are the same as you to come into your life. When those people who differ from us come into our lives, let us appreciate them and celebrate the good in them, see what is good in them, and at long last start to be grateful and rejoice at the fact that between us there are differences, instead of being rude, because they are different from us. In your environment, in your team, there will not always be people like you. As long as you do not realize this you will alienate the very people who are most valuable to you. Learn to accommodate the difference of other people and remember, that their difference is what enriches you.

WE REJECT THOSE WHO ARE DIFFERENT FROM US

As it was argued in the Soviet Union: «You're not like everyone else? So, you're an enemy of the people! You must be judged! »

By the early seventies Annasoltan Kekilova had been quite a successful Soviet woman: a teacher, a journalist, on her shoulders were three published books and her songs and poems were often broadcasted on the radio. Her life as it was could have continued, if not for one event. On the eve of the XXIV Congress of the Communist party, she wrote a couple of letters in which she criticized the Republican leadership. One of the letters was addressed to the Congress, the other to the Committee. As a result of such «reckless» actions, this woman was fired from her job, and her works were banned. This made Kekilova to contact political asylum in the UK.

But to act like this during the Soviet era was dangerous. As a result, 29 – year- old Annasoltan Kekilova was forcibly confined to a psychiatric hospital, Soviet psychiatrics had medical and punitive functions. This Young Turkmenian woman, a gifted journalist, experienced all this firsthand. Until her death, June 19, 1983 she lived in psychiatric hospitals in Aschgabad and Moscow, her books were destroyed, her house was destroyed in a fire of unknown reasons (perhaps it was burnt) with all her scrolls. Most her creative legacy was lost. Her daughter was handed over to an orphanage, without an opportunity to get even secondary education.

All these horrible things happened in the life of Annasoltan Kekilova, who was perfectly healthy before and had never been registered with a psychiatrist. Kekilova's Grandmother could not be indifferent to the fate of her grand-daughter, this elderly woman wrote letters to Moscow to complain about the wrongs perpetrated against her family August 26, 1971: an ambulance which no one ordered and of which there was no need appeared at our home, she a perfectly healthy woman forced, twisting her arms, was pushed into a car and driven to a psychiatric hospital, having rudely shoved her under-aged son to the side. I was told that she was been taking for medical examinations, the doctors in the mental hospital told her she was healthy and they said the following: if you do not give us a personally signed statement that you were crazy and therefore wrote to the Central committee of the Communist party, you will stay in the hospital for eternity ... 9] As they say, the story of the communist party is one of its kind.

In those days, everyone had to be the same, mediocre, not have an opinion and voice. To survive, it was necessary to «keep a low-profile life», to be quiet and keep your head very low, do not have personal opinion, or at least do not voice it out. What happened if you did otherwise, is what we just read in the previous story, dear reader. I can tell you, this is an unhealthy way of building human society. This is not something that will lead us to success. We are not created to be a gray mass, each of us is created to be unique! We need to learn to honor and appreciate the uniqueness of one another, by first noticing the original traits of each person and then respect the investments that they make in the society, due to their unique talents, we allow them to freely demonstrate their gifts and welcome the diversity of these gifts. LET'S STOP SUPPRESSING PEOPLE WHO ARE NOT LIKE US!

Every time you are confronted with people who are different from you, do not declare war on them, don't ridicule them, don't despise them, do not humiliate or belittle them for it. Instead, see wisdom in the fact that you're different and looking at the same things, you see them differently. After all, it is because people are different from you, that in them is concealed something valuable for you, and therefore it is in them we need to seek wisdom. It is those who are different from you, that can enrich you. . People should be appreciated and celebrated for this reason.

Somebody is indignant: *«They behave completely in an unacceptable way!»* But if they did not behave differently, if they were an exact replica of you, then you would not need them, they would not be of any benefit to you. Therefore, that which **distinguishes a person from you, is not a reason to humiliate the him.** That a person is not like you does not give you any reason to belittle his dignity. WHAT DISTINGUISHES A PERSON FROM YOU IS PRECISELY THE REASON TO HONOR THEM. If they are different from you in anything, then that is exactly what makes him unique.

WHAT WE REALLY NEED

- We need someone who is totally different from us

- Only the person who is totally different from you, can truly appreciate you

- Only the person who is different from you, can enrich you

Understand that we do not need our own copy, our «Mini Me « what would we do with them? We do not need to look for people like us! Even in marriage a man and a woman so different from each other are joined together. They are different because they have different functions in marriage: one is designed to carry and bear offspring and therefore looks for stability, safety and security, while the other is designed to protect and provide for his family and is therefore strong, skillful and powerful. It is the distinctions which attract girls and boys together, it's what allows them to create a worthwhile and productive family.

Men and women come together in marriage because they differ from one another. What attracts them to each other? The fact that they differ from each other. No wonder they say: «Opposites attract.» Only the opposite can exalt and enrich each other but under the condition that the strength of the opposite will be recognized. Men and women fall in love because generally we like the opposite, we tend to be drawn to what is clearly different from us.

For example, why does a man marry a certain woman? Prior to proposing to that one woman, for whom he is ready to give his whole being, a man has probably seen many other women, very many different women have come his way during his life journey, there were classmates, neighbors, colleagues. Why did he choose her? Not because she looked like every other woman he met on his way. If she was like a gray mouse, unattractive and with nothing that drew his attention, if she was like every other person around her, then it would have been unlikely that he would notice her. He married her because she was different from those he was used to seeing. HER DIFFERENCE made her stand out from other contenders for his heart and his purse (just kidding!). **People get married because they notice the differences in each other.**

Let's answer the question: why are some women, even though they are beautiful and intelligent still not married? The answer is simple: because each of them has not yet met the man who is able to:

- See her differences

- emphasize them

- honor her differences to the extent that he would be ready to sacrifice himself for her

The reason why one woman or the other has not yet received a marriage proposal from a man prepared to give his heart to her, is that there is yet to be a man who can convince her that he has seen her difference and really appreciates it. Only when a man has gone through all these stages, then and only then, is it worth It for a woman to give him her heart and agree to marry him.

Unmarried girls, listen! Even if you do not remember anything from this book, remember one thing: DO NOT PAY ATTENTION TO ANY MAN WHO DOES NOT SEE YOUR DIFFERENCE. To win your heart, he must convince you that he saw in you that which sets you apart from all the other females. He must not only see the difference from all the other girls, he should highlight and emphasize your differences from all the other girls. He should highlight your differences so that you believe in them! He should convince you of your difference from all the other women in the world! You also must watch after him, to see how much he is willing to sacrifice just to show you that you are different. For the sake of your differences, he must be ready to sacrifice, willing to pay the price. Only then, when the man emphasizes the uniqueness of a woman, that she is special, that he is ready to give his life, his money, ready to give up the comfort zone he is used to do anything for you just because you are different from all the other girls, only then, you can open your heart. Only to such a man can you get married to!

But if the man does not even try to convince you, does not try to prove your difference, is not ready to pay the price, not ready to sacrifice his most precious things, if he does not prove that he is ready to give even his life for you, do not consider such a man as a candidate for marriage. Men like that should be driven far away from you, like filth from a room with a broom, because he is a «tourist»! Who is a «tourist»? This is the one who comes and goes but you do not need «tourists»! You need someone who will take residence in your heart and you in his on a permanent basis.

We need someone who is totally different from us, THAT IS WHY WE NEED TO APPRECIATE WOMEN». Usually men complain, dissatisfied: *«She is impulsive, she is constantly agitated!»* But understand, you men, if she was the same as you without hysterics, without the «impulse « then you would have long been depressed. Imagine you men, that the woman became unemotional, shrewd and logical a complete copy of you, would you prefer her like this?

Perhaps, in some way you would win but smiles would not be in your home. The palette of life is multifaceted, there are many colors, tones and shades. If it were the same color, then you would be depressed, it would not be interesting to live. Therefore, it is inconceivable that a woman is the same as a man!

Or vice versa, women often talk about their future husbands, «No problems, I, will change him, he will become as I need him to be!» But, dear women, if he becomes the way you need him, you would soon realize that you do not need him that way. To confirm this thought I want to use the words of Marlene Dietrich (1901 – 1992), German and American actress and singer, one of the most excellent motion pictures model of women *«Nearly all women want to remake men and when they have achieved this, they lose interest in them.»*

Let us always remember the law of difference! Let us honor and appreciate the differences in people, do not ridicule them for their difference, do not make life difficult for them just for the fact that they are not like you. Those who are different from us is not a tragedy, should not be a problem for us, on the other hand this is for us a discovery, a gift and the most valuable treasure! ONLY THOSE WHO ARE DIFFERENT FROM US, CAN TRULY ENRICH US.

SOMETIMES WE BEGIN TO APPRECIATE SOMETHING – ONLY AFTER WE LOSE IT

Often, we begin to appreciate something - only when we lose it. There are those who did not appreciate what they had and are now biting their elbow meaning they are bitterly regretting their action, the reason- being that such people did not recognize difference and did not take advantage of the wisdom which the basic knowledge of the law of difference provides. Someone, maybe even many of you have heard such stories, that a husband and wife divorced on the fact that they did «not get along?» In truth, it is precisely because of these differences in their nature that they joined together. People divorce not because they did not get along, but because they have not learned to appreciate each other's differences, not learned to respect, they are both different and have not learned to respect the differences of each other.

Apart from this there are other stories: after people got divorced, they were married for a second time, divorced again, and then, remembering their first relationship, decided to give this first marriage a try again. I suggest that most likely these people are thinking: *«But the first marriage in all comparison was better»*. Do you know why such things happen? Because it was the second marriage which gave them the opportunity to see and appreciate appreciate their former spouses from a new perspective, they finally saw the difference, which was the reason they chose each other in the first place. SOMETIMES ONLY HAVING LOST WHAT THEY HAVE PEOPLE START TO APPRECIATE WHAT THEY HAD BEFORE.

For some reason, it is only when we have lost a loved one when the law of difference becomes obviously clear to us. Then we start to really appreciate someone who was close to us.

Vasily Petrovich had just lost his wife. Only now he is painfully aware that many of her qualities, to which he did not pay attention or neglect while she was alive, now became valuable to him. Then those were exactly the things that irritated him, which lead to him to oppress her. How could I have done this to someone whom God gave me and placed next to me? "But now it's too late", regretfully cries the man. Now he would like to turn the time back and build their relationship as she did. Only now Vasily Petrovich saw that during her life-time he did not do everything possible to bring joy to the only love of his life, his wife and thereby bring satisfaction to himself. Now he is certain that their life together would have been much better if he had lived by this rule.

Maria A. was a very gentle, humble and quiet person. Vasily Petrovich says, «I tried to adjust my wife to be like me. I am more agile, responsible, and I tried to remake her, demanded of her that she be the same as me. Now she is gone, and then I suddenly saw how she was a tender, gentle and kind woman. Maybe she was a like she was because of the life experiences she had. Her life could not be said to particularly successful and happy: she raised her only son alone, all her life she worked at the same place and ate at the same table. I demanded of her more action, and now that she's not here, I realized that I possessed a treasure, which I stubbornly refused to notice. Now that I've lost this treasure, I examine every trait of her character as a jewel, and only now all this has become very valuable to me. And now I tremble: I was next to her but for me, something else was more important, I was looking at what was necessary for me, but her values and uniqueness I did not notice. I have trodden with my feet her life, her fragile soul, her originality and uniqueness.»

Vasily Petrovisch did not learn the law of difference on time, for this reason he did not honor, did not value his wife, did not celebrate her during her life time, appreciate and cherish the opportunity to have her all the time near him. Each of you, dear reader, still have time at your advantage. Without wasting time, start appreciating the presence of the people near you today, look closely at them, see and appreciate those differences they possess so that you will not have to see and appreciate those differences only when the people are no more in your life. Do not wait for the moment when you have lost something, when you no more have it, to appreciate it!

The most important gift you can bring to your life and your family this year is to begin to discern the uniqueness, the difference of your spouse, in what way he (she) is unique. There is no person on the earth who does not have something special. If your loved one did not have something remarkable, then you would be the same as them. Begin to discover what differentiates you, start appreciating it and you will see that her (his) value in your eyes will increase. Begin to see and emphasize the virtues that are in other people.

We often see the light only when we lose someone but life should not be like this. THANKS TO WISDOM OUR EYES MUST OPEN. We need to see the light before losing. We do not need to lose something before we see obvious truths. It is known that «the eyes of the wise are in his head» (so is stated in the Bible), this means *wisdom sees.* Seeing differences is the fate of the wise, celebrating differences is the fate of the wise, making compliments is the fate of the wise. When there is no wisdom, we go through life like blind kittens. Only **wisdom allows us to appreciate, see and discern.** Start making compliments, begin to say kind words aloud to them, be thankful that they are around, celebrate and appreciate their difference. We cannot do without wisdom. **ONLY WISDOM PUSHES US TO SEARCH THE UNIQUENESS AND DIFFERENCES OF A PERSON.** Only A wise man looks for differences, only a wise man looks for uniqueness - Do it!

Let's make conclusions Read our chapter

1. **Knowledge of and compliance with the law of difference** helps us to choose a life partner correctly.

2. **If we only communicate with those who are our exact replica,** we impoverish our lives, deprive ourselves of those who really could strengthen and complement us.

3. **If you caught yourself in anyway wishing to get rid of a person,** most likely, you do not want to honor that which distinguishes them from you.

In this chapter, we have looked at what the law of difference claims. We have learned what our natural responses to the differences of other people are:

- *We seek friendship with those who are similar to us*

- *We reject those who are different from us*

Throughout this chapter, we also dealt the fact of what we really need. In the next chapter, we will look at what dangers awaits us if we are reluctant to notice people. If we pass by people without noticing them, we are missing the most important thing in life, and then it becomes too poor and colorless.

GOLDEN TRUTHS

The law of difference is the ability to discern the difference in people, their gifts, potentials and ability

The law helps to understand the differences between men and women, thus allowing to understand and honor the role of each

We are attracted to what is different from us

What makes you different from others is that which makes you unique

Never seek where you are similar to others

That which is exactly the same as you, does not enrich you

Only what is different from you, can complement you

Whomever is just like you, will never strengthen you, will not be able to complement you and will not be able to enrich you

Anytime you are confronted with people who are different from you, do not declare war on them, don't be rude to them, do not humiliate or belittle them for it

SELF-ASSESSMENT

1. When you see a person, who is not like you...

1) You reject them (0).

2) You have trouble with such people (1)

3) Try to make friends with them and do make friends(2)

2. Do you welcome the differences that exist between men and women?

1) No (0)

2) Partly (1)

3) Yes (2)

3. What do look for in people when you first meet?

1) where we are similar (0)

2) what would be easy to put up with (1)

3) where we are radically different from each other (2)

EVALUATION OF TEST RESULTS

(0 points) We're sorry, your life is completely at odds with the law of differences, you are living contrary to it. You are looking for friendship only with those who are like you, and completely reject those who are different from you. Therefore, you find it hard to be respectful towards

other people. Because you do not discern the difference in others, you are creating problems for yourself and deprive yourself of the wealth that is hidden in everyone who happens to come your way along the path of life. If you have a desire to change then continue to study this book. The recommendations it contains will help you change your life qualitatively!

(1 - 5 points) Not bad, you want to ensure that to you practice the law of difference in your life. You try to notice where one person is different from another. It helps you see the difference between one person's gifts and that of the other people, this means you are aware and appreciate the uniqueness of each person. Appreciating the people around you, you create around you a life full of light, love and harmony. Continue in this direction! You will continue to inspire others to do the same. This book will help you.

(6 points) Congratulations! Using your ability to discern and appreciate the differences of other people, you attract all the wealth that is close to you because of these people. This will enrich not only your life but will also make richer the world around you. You have enough wisdom to appreciate those who are not like you. You are not afraid to make yourself uncomfortable accepting those different from you. I invite you to share with others what you have perfectly learned.

GUIDELINES FOR THE IMPLEMENTATION OF PRACTICAL TASKS

1. CAUTION: These activities should not only be read and forgotten, they are VERY IMPORTANT. According to many years of working with people I know people often perform such tasks «for the sake of it" but it's your life, this is for you, take them seriously.

2. To maximize results, I suggest performing the tasks within the 24 hours, otherwise, you will forget, get distracted and you will distance yourself from the results you want.

3. To answer all the questions, find a quiet place and systematically work out the tasks.

4. Meditate on each chapter, on all the points that you underlined for yourself, reflect on the them and write out your steps of action.

5. Set yourself a time frame, constraints, to help you not to put off working on yourself.

6. Find someone you can be accountable to, who could help remind you to stay focused on working on yourself.

PRACTICAL TASKS

Analyze what kind of people you choose for friendship and communication, those like you or those who are different from you? What does this mean (perhaps a desire for comfort, etc.)? What are you planning to review in your relationships, in your choice of companion, friends and acquaintances in communication?

What is your reaction to the differences of other people? Do you reject those who are different from you? Prove it with examples from your own life. What do we really need? Do you really need people who are your copy? How does this principle apply to marriage?

Which principles should guide you in choosing your future spouse? What should every girl dreaming of getting married remember? If you are married, answer the question: why did he marry you? Why did you agree to his advances? If you are married, or just going to get married, why did you chose only this man?

CHAPTER 5

WHAT HAPPENS IF YOU DO NOT NOTICE PEOPLE?

WHAT HAPPENS IF YOU DO NOT NOTICE PEOPLE?

I recall, dear reader, that in the previous chapter we talked about what the law of differences claims. In this chapter, you will learn what the consequences are when we are reluctant to notice the people, what we lose when we just pass by, without paying any attention to them. If we pass by a person without noticing his or her:

- Differences
- uniqueness,

this means that we are blind, we cannot see

that **"position of influence"**, that person could serve us, if we honored them,

also, that which we could learn from them.

This shows says that we lack wisdom. If we:

- we do not see each other's differences
- pass by each other
- do not stop to honor each other
- do not take something useful from each other,

it indicates a lack of wisdom.

IF PEOPLE FOR US, LOOK THE SAME

For the ordinary person, all people have one face.

- Blaise Pascal (1623 - 1662), French mathematician, physicist, writer and philosopher

When I came to the USSR, I often heard from the Soviet people the following phrase: «all Africans look the same!» The same is often said about the Chinese and other representatives of the Mongoloid race. How can all people be «one face» that is, devoid of individual, significant differences; identical, very similar to each other? [10]

Experiments conducted by American scientists led by Michael Bernstein of the University of Miami, helped discover the cause of this phenomenon. It turned out that the inability to recognize representatives of other races is that people «subconsciously» prefer to divide into "ours and theirs" however, the representatives of «their» group (racial, etc.) They will easily recognize much better. [11]

We have based our prejudices and our perception of the world on accepted norms (for more details about this in the seventh chapter) and stereotypes, classify people, defining thereby people with whom we prefer to communicate and those who do not fit into the framework of the standards we have created. As a result, we do not have the wisdom to differentiate the representative of "one race" from another, for example one African from another African. This is not because all Africans look the same or have one face but because the person who says so, does not have the wisdom, knowledge, skills or desire to distinguish between the representatives of this race. The ability to distinguish is formed with the help of skills, knowledge and understanding and all these are properties of wisdom.

We can see the consequences of this. According to surveys of sociologists, almost half (44%) of the St. Petersburg school do not want to be friends with someone of another nationality and do not want to know about other folks. These studies suggest that on the average teenagers from the ages of 12 to 18 years can name only 3-6 maximum of the 12 nationalities of people living in St. Petersburg. The worst thing is that some of the young residents generally do not want to know about other peoples, they say, "don't I have anything better to do than to study them?". Among the non-standard responses are also found the following: «what is the difference? They all have one face" [12].

Intolerance towards others that are different from us are cultivated during childhood. This is evidenced by the massive detention of underaged youths during the «Russian March», the participation of adolescents in the beatings and even the murder of people of non - Slavic appearance. The reason for this behavior is often the belief that the youths cultivate, based on the" kitchen talks" in the parents' home, also the influence of media, which in a specific way broadcast information about events in Biryulyovo, «Russian Marches» and raids in the markets.

There are teenagers who understand the word «extremism» to mean «murder» and «love for the motherland.» As a means of "inoculation" against inter-racial conflicts partakers, the survey suggests the following, apart from the strict obedience of Russian laws and respect to Russians,» do not poke your nose in someone else's business», «depot whoever deserves to be «, «behave yourself calmly «, «live in your homeland «. As a radical means curbing the immigration of "non - Russians" a considerable part of the 15-18 year-olds, did not think twice to suggest a "global cleansing " [12] Is this state of affairs in society not enough to provide a cause for concern? There are similar uprisings all around the world. In America, there are young people still becoming part of "white superiority" movements. In both subtle and obvious ways, racism exists still and is a result of a lack of wisdom. As educator and anti-racism activist, Jane Elliott says, "prejudice is an emotional commitment to ignorance." Elliott conducted an experiment after the assassination of Martin Luther King Jr. with her third-grade class in Riceville, Iowa which was 98% white people. Through her experiment, "blue eye brown eye", separating the class by distinction of their eye color, she concluded that once people were separated by their difference, kids who had been friends all year long, became enemies, kids who had formerly treated each other with respect, began to tear each other down, as a result of not embracing their difference. As a result of this experiment, these kids were changed for a life time. There is documentary called "A Class Divided" where you can see firsthand the impact of the experiment.

WE PASS PEOPLE WITHOUT NOTICING THEM

Yesterday, the lights were turned off. Two hours spent without Internet, had fellowship with my family. As it turned out - they are very nice people!

Joke (unknown)

I have noticed that in our culture people often live without noticing anyone around. They do not see people, look at them but at the same time manage to ignore. What does it mean «not to see a person at point - blank?» According to the dictionary of Russian synonyms, it means: to look down on him, as from a high bell tower, not to give any significance, show no willingness to know, ignore, take for granted, do not notice, pay no attention, relate with contempt, despise, look down on, attach no value to. [13]

One psychoanalytic at a wedding ceremony conducted an experiment. Standing close to the hosts, he watched through the terrace and realized that none of the hosts listened to what the guests said. Then he joined the stream of visitors and going to one of the hosts, said quietly:

- Today, my grandmother died.
The host said:
- How beautiful, how cute!
He said the same thing to another host, and he replied:

- How nice of you!
And the bridegroom answered and said:
- Old man, it's time that you follow. [14]

Unfortunately, this happens with us very often with us. We welcome people, ask them how are you and run away, not waiting for an answer. We do not notice their distinctive features and characteristics, the most that we know are the names of people. For us it's just a name, something that helps us to recognize, distinguish one from another, just as we distinguish between inanimate objects: I-pad, pen, note book, a spool of thread, and in a similarly way we treat people: "this is Charles and this is Sue ....." It's such a trivial attitude to people, it becomes downright scary. You should not look at people this way! [9]

Few people think about these things. For example, you find yourself in a room with lots of people, like fifty people, what do you see? Some do not see anything, some sees only them self, some see people in general, «Well, people are gathered» (a feeling of indifference) but no one can see an individual person. When we enter a room full of people, we rarely think of others. Usually, the average person does not discern, who is who, how he dressed, hairstyle, color of eyes, what they can say, what interesting thing they have to offer, what color eyes or hair, what kind of clothes, which color, how beautiful, most of us are not so observant.

---

[9] *Trivial - a very simple, banal. Triviality - extreme degree of simplification.*

Sometimes we can't even remember people with whom we sat just an hour or two ago, for us they are just a colorful dot and wear things like, "aaa! yes someone sat near me, someone in red,» for us the person was only a color, we could not remember the neither the face nor his personality.

Here is demonstrative dialogue from the film «If Only» (Melodrama with fantastic assumptions in 2004 directed by Gil Dzhangera):

- Maybe I should give a red cashmere sweater as a gift?
- he has one of his own. He wore it the last time he came here, and all the time spoke about how he liked it.
- and where was I?
- you stood close by

That is, we pathologically do not know how to recognize humans as humans. In my observations, the way we describe people: «white girl», «girl in black», «that red haired person,» or, «that Russian» or, «the plump», «the slender», «that fast one», "the one that is always active" or "the quiet one", this is how we perceive people.

If we are in an audience, we think more of ourselves: «Look at me, I am so handsome!» People care more about how to impress others, to draw more attention to themselves. Most often we do not notice others, we do not see their dignity, their advantages, do not pay attention to what they have better than us, do not analyze why they are who they are. For us the most important thing is that we be seen and heard. Have you ever thought about this? **The ability to honor people is not inherent in our culture.**

TO IGNORE PEOPLE IS TO IGNORE THE COLORS OF LIFE

As the colorblind people say- life is like the rainbow: made of black bands, and white bands.
- Anecdote from the life of the color - blind

Not all the inhabitants of the earth equally perceive the whole palette of diversity, which differentiates us. Color perception in humans is different. For example, the inability to distinguish between one or more colors called is called **daltonism (colorblindness).** Colorblind people can see well, but perceive the colors of the surrounding world differently than other people, they are unable to correctly identify certain colors, as a result, they are disadvantaged. **To adequately perceive the world and receive all the joy and benefits, you must have the ability to fully see.**

Therefore, people who are not able to correctly identify the different ranges of colors:

- cannot enjoy the wealth of colors around them
- cannot, for example, distinguish between the colors on traffic lights

- more than 150 professions are prohibited for them

A person who cannot differentiate all the color the world has to display, misses a lot in life.

But there is another kind of «color blindness». There are people that are similar to the colorblind, the only difference is that they do not notice the wealth of every person. At best, these people perceive others in general, not seeing the details of their uniqueness. In the worst instance, they see others simply as a crowd. **Anyone who does not notice the differences of colors, loses a lot in life, but even more at a loss is one who does not notice the uniqueness of each person.**

Let me ask you a question: how many people did you have time today to compliment? For the whole day, you did not see a single person on whom it was possible to draw your attention? Not a single beautifully made up woman? Not a single well and tastefully dressed man? There was no one person who had a beautiful hairstyle? How could you manage to live a whole day without uttering a compliment?

The fact that we do not compliment people and do not say good words to people, means that, in our society something is out of order and if this continues, we will run into trouble. This occurs from the fact that we were not taught to see the differences. The inability to see the difference in people around us makes us blind. More than that, if we fail to notice the peculiarities of other people, we will not see the most important things in life. ALL THE MOST IMPORTANT THINGS IN LIFE ARE IN THE DETAILS, IN LITTLE THINGS. If you can walk past a woman with beautiful hair, good makeup, dressed tastefully and did not notice anything at all then you are unable to see and perceive anything. This means that you are not able to recognize difference.

If we cannot see the external differences between people that which is attractive, that which grabs your eye, things like hairstyle, makeup, clothing, then what can we say about internal values of humans, such as kindness, confidence, elegance, friendliness, generosity all not visible to the naked eye. These things are hidden, mostly deep inside, you need to make an effort, otherwise they cannot be easily noticed. If we do not notice the obvious how can we then see what is hidden to the human eye. If we do not notice beautiful hair or an unusual color or shape of the eyes, then how can we observe the internal qualities which are much more valuable than those external expressions?

Once you stop making compliments, you stop seeing and noticing the colors of life. Complimenting OTHERS should become the norm for us, this is what gives you the confirmation that you see the differences in other people and that you not only see this difference but that you also honor and celebrate those differences in others that you distinguish and recognize. When you make compliments to other people, then you are enriched!

To ignore people is to refuse to see the colors of life, and if you stop seeing the colors of life, then your life becomes gray and dull. THE BRIGHTEST COLORS OF LIFE: ARE PEOPLE. We are all different from each other. One person differs from another, as one star differs from another, so one has a different hair color, eye color and face configuration than the others. In this uniqueness and diversity of each person on earth is hidden all the colors and the beauty of this world. IF YOU STOP NOTICING PEOPLE THEN YOU STOP NOTICING THE COLORS OF LIFE. What are the colors of life? It is the specificity of the character, temperament, delicate quality of soul, which, like diamonds should delight our soul and eyes, which are the flowers that should fill our hearts with joy and happiness. To see them is not so simple. It requires skill and the ability to see the depth and details, also being scrupulous is necessary. Personally, I love to observe people, listen to them watch them. I like to explore all the features of the variety and differences that people represent. That's what saves me from depression. I do not like it when people standing next to me being silent. I want to find what is inside of them, what they are filled and what is their internal content. I'm curious to hear how they think, talk, what conclusions they make, what questions interests them. To stop seeing the colors of life, I tell you, implies to live for yourself, and then you, dear reader, definitely will encounter a problem: your own care for yourself can exceed any allowable level, immersing you into a depression, and then mental disorder awaits you.

If you stopped noticing the colors of life, you have ceased to live. If someone has it good, even better than you be happy with them! If someone has things going worse than you then sympathize with them! This is also the colors of life. If you cannot distinguish who is worse, and who is better, it means that you only see yourself and seeing only you means you see nothing. Darkness, darkness, and then a psychiatric hospital.

IGNORING PEOPLE, WE LIVE EGOCENTRIC

Why can we ignore the uniqueness of other people? People do not see the uniqueness, the differences of others and their «rainbow» when they are:

- *fixed only on themselves*
- *see only their own problems*
- *think only of their imperfections*

Such people are self - centered and selfishness. This is the first cause of human poverty.

Selfishness, is the reason of self-destruction. There is no worse defect in the human soul than selfishness, self-pity and self-centeredness. The earliest manifestation of selfishness is self-pity. If a person lives, concentrating on them self and their problems, they are not able to see other people. I can tell you, why this is dangerous: the reason why people end in a psychiatric hospital lies in the fact that they are centered and focused only on themselves. If a person lives only for his problems, focused only on them, it will lead first to depression, and then to schizophrenia.

Everyone who meets you on the path of life, was designed by God to enrich you. But if you do not notice the differences of other people or refuse to honor and celebrate them, then you are risking simply to "drown in your problems", in the daily vanities of life, in these rat races that the system of this world forces on us. When you do not want to notice the difference of other people, or do not want to honor and celebrate them, then you are declaring that you care only for yourself and this is egoism in its clearest form. The more a person thinks about himself, the more he is «drowning» in his problems and difficulties. Therefore, 'a priori', do not think about yourself. Only people belonging to the biomass think only about themselves.[10]

A healthy person pays attention to and thinks about them self only 20% of their time. 80% OF THE TIME, WE SHOULD THINK ABOUT OUR GOALS AND ABOUT HOW TO IMPROVE LIVES OF OTHERS, OR WHAT ONE CAN LEARN FROM THEM. Such a healthy person was Mother Teresa of Calcutta, who took on the mission of caring for the dying poor in the streets of Calcutta, India.

---

[10] A priori, (. a priori - literally «from the) — knowledge of the Heart to experience and independently of it, in a figurative sense - without relying on the knowledge of facts without checking, without any proof.

She left the walls of the monastery, to live among the poor and help them.

A healthy person pays attention to and thinks about them self only 20% of their time. 80% OF THE TIME, WE SHOULD THINK ABOUT OUR GOALS AND ABOUT HOW TO IMPROVE LIVES OF OTHERS, OR WHAT ONE CAN LEARN FROM THEM. Such a healthy person was Mother Teresa of Calcutta, who took on the mission of caring for the dying poor in the streets of Calcutta, India. She left the walls of the monastery, to live among the poor and help them.

The first woman, this nun picked up in the mud-drenched street, was gnawed by rats and ants. All hospitals refused to accept her, the only one, who did not give up on the unfortunate woman, was Mother Teresa. She served in the slums of Calcutta those people who had nothing or no one. Those to whom no one wanted to come near because of the stench and the bugs on them. This nun went to those who did not have even the strength to ask for alms, those who did not have even rags to cover their body, to those who could not sit due to physical depletion, those who expected their death there directly on the streets. [13]

Mother Teresa did not live for herself and her and problems, she dedicated her life to the people. Looking around her, she saw people who needed her help, whose situations were worse than her own. She voluntarily gave up any form of personal comfort. One of the journalists who managed to become a witness of how this nun daily, selflessly, cared for the lepers and the dying, said: «Would you stop doing it for a million dollars?" Do you know, dear reader, how Mother Teresa answered? «for even more than a million and I would not stop doing it", she said, "this love is free of charge out of love for Christ! [16]"

Why did this woman say such things? Because she saw value in every human being. People tried to convince her that she is committed to treating not the cause but a consequence, only «patch holes». She was told that her work will drown in the ocean of problems that can only be solved at the state level. However, she continued to do it, not counting her efforts as anything but small or insignificant. She saw in these needful and unfortunate people, just as in all others, more «decent» people who also have the right to love, compassion, and acceptance, mercy, with the right to be accepted and recognized as people, created in the image and likeness of God. If Jesus died for all, because he sees the value of each person, if God's son was not ashamed to die for people who are small and insignificant compared to him, to die for their sins, then all the more we should be looking for the people around us to value and appreciate them. We need to dedicate our lives to serve them and help solve their problems.

When you do not live only for yourself, when you are not exclusively devoted to you, when all your thought life is not exclusively devoted to you, then you do notice negative emotions, they no longer control you, you do not worry

about what destructive thoughts will fall on your head today. As a result, you will experience constant growth, instead of constantly complaining about failure. When you see someone else apart from you, then your world is no longer narrow, it is large enough to notice people, to see and receive their differences. When you do not live self - centered lives, then you are truly a healthy person.

THE PERSON WHO DOESN'T SEE ADVANTAGES IN OTHERS, LIVES A POOR LIFE

The greatest poverty – is poverty of the heart.

- Mother Teresa (1910 - 1997),
a Roman Catholic nun and
Nobel Peace Prize Winner

When we do not notice the differences in people, we are impoverished, just as much as we see nothing good in people. HE WHO DOES NOT NOTICE THE WEALTH HIDDEN IN OTHER PEOPLE, IS A POOR PERSON.

- *Not noticing external beauty, we cannot enjoy it*

- *Not noticing a person's knowledge, we cannot learn from them*

- *Not seeing wisdom, we do not get the necessary advice*

- Not noticing and noting the abilities of a person, we will not be able to use them

- Not noticing a person's sense of humor, we can't improve our mood thanks to their subtle jokes

In every person, there is something special something that I do not have that can enrich me, if only I can identify these differences in the other person. If I do not see them, then I remain a poor and a constantly depressed person. **The richest people are those who look for the differences in others who surround them: in all whom they meet on their way in life.** If you set the task to find these differences in people, you are immediately enriched. Disregarding the differences of others, you remain the same as you are - roughly speaking, poor. Many are impoverished because of their inability to see what they can be enriched with because of differences which are abundant in others.

A person will become poorer when he ceases to:

- notice the uniqueness, «colors» of people

- give people compliments

Not seeing the uniqueness of others, thinking only about ones' problems and not noticing the uniqueness of people around us, we become poor because we do not see the features of wisdom, knowledge, beauty, and cannot make use of them, cannot take advantage of them we feel that we are crushed under the weight of our problems depressed psychologically and spiritually.

For example, I do not have depression. You want to know why? I not only see people around me but their features. I see details and nuances, even little things about them. That's why I do not see grayness, but rather a rainbow palette of colors that is in every man. When I get into an audience, then I embrace the whole room looking and seeing each person individually. Whenever I get the chance, I always interest myself in knowing individual people: «Hello! How are you? What are You doing?», I am interested in knowing what's inside of this person, I want to hear it, especially if the first time I see him, I want to know his unique story. If I have a chance to talk with another person, I can't sit standoffish, without noticing them. I want to be «enriched» by them, I want to know how they live, what is inside of them, why is they are so beautiful, why they are so elegant, how they feel.

I look forward in expectation to every man as a vast ocean of treasures, that is not accessible to me and I want to find different ways, find an inlet, to open up this unknown world to me, that this person shares their hidden treasures with me. If I look at a person, I feel and see one kind of beauty, if I look at another I see another kind of beauty. I am captivated by the beauty and uniqueness of others, I am drawn by the specific qualities of others, I am enriched when I hear about the lives of others, what they live for. I would like to meet with everybody! Therefore, whenever an audience gathers, I ask people to introduce themselves, I ask them: «what is your name? Who are you? Where are you from? How are you? What are you doing? Where were you? What is happening in your life? When I interact with people I invite everyone to speak out, I am happy to listen to people.

I am completely enriched and saturating by the uniqueness of each. The more people I see, the more my life displays the rainbow, which consists of a wealth of different colors. I am very interested in discovering and admiring every color of this rainbow, I am always fascinated by people, each person individually. Giving people recognition, compliments, glory, recognizing and celebrating the uniqueness of each, I discover God's wealth. This is the principle of my life, and this is how I manage to live without depression. BEGIN TO SEE A RAINBOW IN PEOPLE!

How often do you go near people, to get to know them, get acquainted with them? I know that these questions trouble people. «Why do this?» They ask. Most people do not think they should be interested and inquire about other people's lives. We are more interested in people only when we need them for some reason. Is this true? If we seek to communicate with people only when we need them, when we can get something valuable for ourselves, if we are not interested in other people to touch their rich inner world, then we are truly poor people! If you are not interested in other people and listening to them, if you are only interested in yourself and sharing only your news, then you are a poor person! If you are sitting in a company where a lot of people are and there is not an urge in you to go and meet someone new and ask questions, or just talk to someone then you are a poor man. You are pathologically not interested in other people, this is not because it is not part of your culture, it's more personal, it is not part of your values.

The reason why we so often do not, lies in the fact that people do not embody for us, valuable. This means that first, we do not value ourselves and therefore another person cannot be of any value to us. When we do not value ourselves, we do not believe that we can enrich others through our fellowship. In the same way, we do not believe that anyone can enrich our lives. Man is not our first value. Goals, achievements, how we can impress others, what impressions have people made on us but not the person them self. This means that you focus only on yourself and live entirely egoistic. **The person who doesn't see advantages in others, lives a poor life.**

TO IGNORE THE DIFFERENCES OF PEOPLE IS DANGEROUS

Dear reader, I want to tell you one important THOUGHT: **to ignore the difference in people is much more dangerous than it may seem at first glance.** To ignore the differences of other people, to stay blind to their uniqueness leads to the neglect of this person. If you do not notice the person, it means that they are a blank space for you. This is a small part of the problem. Secondly, a habit of not noticing the differences of other people leads to much worse consequences.

The question to you: how many people did you have time today to make a compliment? If your answer is «zero», it means that you have not developed the ability to see. Most likely today, you have seen someone with a new hairstyle, someone with cute make-up, you passed by someone who was tastefully dressed. This was more than enough to notice a person but you did not! Not only that, you also were not noticed! While you were trying to look very good: smartly dressed, fabulous makeup, styled your hair, etc., nobody even noticed. Do you know why nobody complimented you today? Because we are blind: we see only ourselves, "the loved one"! Do you know what this is called? Selfishness! It is the worst of all human vices.

When you do not compliment other people, it says you are focused on yourself, on your problems, you are not cheerful, you do not appreciate others other people, you do not celebrate the victories and successes of others. Therefore, you are immersed in yourself, and that means that you have a problem! We have said that when a person is immersed in them self and live exclusively for their problems, it will drive you crazy and place you in a psychiatric hospital.

There are two causes of schizophrenia or insanity. The first reason is self-centeredness. If I do not notice other's differences, it says I only for my problems: everything is bad, "I feel bad, I hurt all over, nobody loves me, I, I, I.....". It means that a person does not see the colors of the world, one sees only them self and is fixed exclusively on the negative. This can lead to depression and then before long,

the person starts to hear voices in their head. This is the first reason of insanity.

The second reason of insanity is when a person is too carried away by himself, this person is of the impression that nothing around him exists, the right to exist has only one person himself. In fact, such a person says, «*I am the center of the universe! Let everything revolve around me!*".

Therefore, people who are crazy are either focused on them self, or excessively aggressive. The second is people who are overexcited by their own glory, they see only themselves and no one else around. A person like that does not see life, does not see that somebody feels bad, that someone has a harder life than them, or does not see that someone has good things going because he sees only them self. Therefore, a crazy person is either always laughing, which is one category of madness, or angry, those who are depressed. Both issues arise from too much concentration on oneself.

You cannot live by yourself! No matter how bad you might feel, no matter how many problems you might have, there is always someone worse off than you are. You should not live by yourself in self-centeredness and think only of yourself. I repeat, this is the worst way to live, which can be dangerous to us and our mental well-being. If you do not make compliments, if you do not see others, if you do not notice the difference of others, you don't know why you should give compliments to a person: "she looks good, has such a good smile, he is so friendly and kind", and you do not see all this! - If you do not see what other people notice, if you do not see anybody, then you are already on the way to a mental hospital, the psychiatrists are waiting for you!

Making compliments to people should not be for the sake of others, we need to do it for ourselves: for me, it is the prevention of schizophrenia. Begin to see the colors of life! When you see the colors of life, you can't be « fixed « on yourself. When you are constantly celebrating others, you will not live exclusively for yourself. You do not face the danger of depression and wallow in your problems if you are constantly making compliments and celebrating others. Go ahead and start to notice other people! This is an excellent prevention of depression and schizophrenia.

If someone smiles at you, tell them they have a good smile. If they have beautiful hair, give them a compliment. Even if you've seen it before, still tell them that they are the first person that has come your way with such amazing hair. It will not be a lie, because you are emphasizing the uniqueness of that person. If a person has a good face or a friendly look, tell him about it! If anyone helped an elderly person, or forgets not to call their mother, grandmother - praise them for it! If somebody paved a way for you, offered you place then tell the person, how good a heart they have, because they noticed your need, your discomfort and found the strength in them self to help you, to do something good for you. Doesn't such an act by a person deserve to be seen and marked? Just start to open your mouth and pronounce pleasant and encouraging words to other people!

Set a goal to constantly notice the differences of people and give them compliments. Begin to be interested in other people. In this way, you will heal yourself from all of what I wrote above. This is the prevention of schizophrenia. The fact that you notice people and make compliments, you are doing yourself good and you preventing mental disorder, with simple words you can reduce the risk of going mad.

Do not worry that no one will notice you that no one will make compliments to you. As stated in a wise book, it is more blessed to give than to receive. When you give compliments, your goodness, your positives to people, when you are happy with those who have some success or achievement, when you're compassionate to those who are now in a worse situation than you, you improve your health, your mental and moral state.

You remember, dear reader, the words of Blaise Pascal, whose words I have used as an epigraph to this chapter? He argues that: «*to the ordinary people all humans look alike.*» If we pass by people without noticing them, according to Pascal, we are ordinary people, that is, we do not stand out, we are not living an excellent or exceptional life. The mediocre life has this property of tending to be like every other person, not standing out, be average. If such a trait is still in us we must put an end to it. [11]

---

[11] *Mediocre - worthless, no outstanding person.*

We should learn to live by keeping the law of difference, which is reflected honoring every individual person, because in them is hidden a whole world which in favorable conditions can generously enrich us. We should be outstanding personalities, an important attribute of which is the ability to manifest exceptional abilities, stand out among others, be the first among equals. Only outstanding personality have a specific life purpose and as a result have a big heart, to see and notice the people around him.

Let's make conclusions of this chapter

1. Only to ordinary and mediocre man do all people seem to have one face. The knowledge and application of the law difference will help you get rid of this problem.

2. To be blind enough to ignore people, means not to be wise.

3. To live only for your problems, ignoring the presence of others, is dangerous in that it can lead to spending the rest of ones' life in a psychiatric hospital.

So, dear reader, we have finished with you a study of another chapter of the book «The Law of Difference». In it, we looked at the disastrous consequences which can result in the inability or unwillingness to notice people. When we pass by people without noticing them, we are missing themost important thing in life and are poor. In general,

we understand that to not notice people is dangerous. The next chapter of this book is proof that everybody is a «star.» We will learn with you, dear reader, what the component of the «star» of every person is their uniqueness, originality and value. Also, we will look at some questions which might seem controversial to our perception:

- Can you see a «star» in the other person?

- Is it enough to recognize only a «star» in the other person?

- What could be the reaction to a «star»?

As they say on TV: «Stay with us!» The «stars» are waiting for us, exactly which ones? you will learn in the next chapter of this book, the law of difference.

GOLDEN TRUTHS

The ability to discern difference is formed through the help of skills, knowledge and understanding, all which are properties of wisdom

It is so tragic, so pathetic that we were not taught to perceive people as humans

Once you stop making compliments, you stop seeing the colors of life

If you stop noticing people, you no longer notice the colors of life

If you stop noticing the colors of life, then you have stopped living

Anyone who does not notice the wealth hidden in others is a poor person

To ignore the differences in people is much more dangerous than it may seem at first glance

SELF – ASSESSMENT

1. How focused are you on yourself?

1) In a large way (0)

2) Relatively small (1)

3) to A lesser extent (2)

2.To be self-centered is….

1)a healthy care of myself, do not see anything wrong in it (0)

2) If you don't think about yourself no one will (1)

3) the worst of vices, that can be in people (2)

3. How often do you make compliments to people?

1) Never (0)

2) Sometimes, when possible (1)

3) several times in a day (2)

4. How often do you go to people, to get to know them?

1) Never, why do I have to? (0)

2) Occasionally but I force myself to do it (1)

3) Constantly, I do it easily and with great pleasure because people are interesting to me (2)

5. How often are you in depression?

    1) Often, almost always (0)

    2) Sometimes, rarely (1)

    3) Never; I don't know what it is (2)

6. How observant are you?

    1) Not observant at all (0)

    2) To an average extent (1)

    3) No detail escapes my attention (2)

EVALUATION OF TEST RESULTS

(0 - 4 points) We're sorry, you are characterized by the reluctance and inability to notice the people around you. It indicates the absence of the ability to observe and also a pathological inability to perceive people as individuals. If you are interested in people it's usually when your personal interest is involved. As soon as you gain a benefit from a person you forget about them. Facing an audience, you are more likely to think about how to make an impression, how to attract attention to yourself. Making compliments is so alien to you that you feel uncomfortable doing it. You should keep in mind the dangers posed by selfishness and all its manifestations. It is unnecessary to continue to live a poor life, when noticing others can enrich you more than you can ever dream or imagine. Stop being «color - blind» through life! Acquire wisdom and begin to see and notice people all around you!

(5 - 11 points) Not bad, you already notice the gaps in your ability honor other people. The good news is that you do not remain indifferent to this and seek to change the status quo. Even if you do not tend to pay attention to people you are working to overcome this, to become more responsive, proactive and sensitive to the needs of others. You sincerely strive for the attainment of wisdom, so you won't remain blind to the colors of life that are so rich in the world around us. You need to develop the ability to see and recognize the advantages of people, their positives, where they excel. Learn to do an analysis of who they are and why they are what they are, or have achieved the success that you are still dreaming of.

(12 points) Congratulations! Most likely, you do not even know depression and the world is continuously pouring out before you, all the colors of the rainbow. This is not surprising. You are a person who keeps their eyes open when it comes to people and their differences. The uniqueness of each person enriches and nourishes you, so that you never stay «hungry» but are always fulfilled. You have many friends and a large circle of acquaintances. Most importantly, you do not neglect people and this is what makes communication with you so enjoyable, that all people, without exception, are pleased to meet you.

GUIDELINES FOR THE IMPLEMENTATION OF PRACTICAL TASKS

1. CAUTION: These activities should not only be read and forgotten, they are VERY IMPORTANT. According to many years of working with people I know people often perform such tasks «for the sake of it" but it's your life, this is for you, take them seriously.

2. To maximize results, I suggest performing the tasks within the 24 hours, otherwise, you will forget, get distracted and you will distance yourself from the results you want.

3. To answer all the questions, find a quiet place and systematically work out the tasks.

4. Meditate on each chapter, on all the points that you underlined for yourself, reflect on the them and write out your steps of action.

5. Set yourself a time frame, constraints, to help you not to put off working on yourself.

6. Find someone you can be accountable to, who could help remind you to stay focused on working on yourself.

PRACTICAL TASKS

Rate your level of focus on yourself and your problems on a scale of 0 to 10, where 0 is the minimum value and 10 the maximum. What conclusions can you draw about yourself? If you rate yourself low, what are consequences? What are you going to do to change the current situation?

On the average, how many people a day do you compliment? If your figures are low, what does this mean? What can this lead to? What do you need to do to increase this figure?

Develop an action plan how you can be interested the people you meet every day of your life? Write out for yourself the methods and techniques, how will you do this and at what frequency? Give yourself a goal to increase the number of people with whom you plan to communicate positively with each day.

CHAPTER 6

EVERYBODY IS A "STAR"

EVERYBODY IS A "STAR"

In the previous chapter, we looked at what happens when we do not notice people. In this chapter, we're going to emphasize the fact that each person is a "Star". We will consider issues such as uniqueness, originality and the value of each person. We will seek answers to uncomfortable questions for us such as:

- *Are you able to recognize the «stars» in the people around you?*
- *Is it enough only to recognize the «star» in the other person, or is something more required?*
- *How do you develop the correct response to the «star»?*

We say that every person deserves respect, because each of us is unique, unique and interesting. That is why every person:
husband
wife
parents
each of our friends
chief
waiter
driver
boy next door etc.,
is a «star».

To notice other people is the same thing as seeing «stars» in others. HE WHO IS NOT ABLE TO RECOGNIZE THE «STAR» IN OTHER, LIVES IN DARKNESS. Just like in the physical life the night sky without the moon and without stars is a complete darkness, in the same way a person who is not able to discern the difference of others, is living in darkness. what does the darkness in our lives mean? This darkness is called «self-centeredness.» This means that a person who is not able to notice the differences of others and honor their them lives exclusively for their problems and is obsessed by them self.

A unique combination of external and internal qualities of a person is wealth. Everyone has different knowledge. Therefore, each person is a treasure trove. Not everyone however is able to recognize and discover it.

Each person is:
- *Special*
- *Interesting*
- *valuable*

Every person has their own differences and «colors». Please note how God created the world. His created world has a huge variety all things:
- *different continents*
- *climate*
- *nature*
- *people*

All this together creates a bright, colorful, rich picture of the world around us. If you remove at least one of these thing, the world becomes smaller and poorer. The same goes for people they are a variety of jewelry. When we understand that each person is:

Unique
interesting
filled with hidden wealth

then we see people around us not as a general group or crowd but as a variety of jewelry. Everyone is a «star», we only need to learn to recognize the «star» in each person! Learn to see, what to celebrate, what to compliment people for and then you will not have any more questions about what you can celebrate in other people.

EACH PERSON IS UNIQUE AND ORIGINAL

In each person is hidden a bell and when touched, the person gives the best sounds that he has.

- Maxim Gorky (1868 - 1936),
the Russian writer, novelist, playwright

Is this not a truly interesting statement? These words mean that no matter how ordinary and similar to one another people may seem on the outside, the most important thing is hidden inside them. This invisible treasure sometimes imperceptible to the naked eye, but if all the necessary conditions for it to be disclosed are met then it can fill the world with its remarkable and unique music. «Bells», this is the uniqueness of the person, which is designed to enrich the whole world. What is hidden inside is designed to come out to reveal its beauty to the outside world and not be buried forever in the hustle and bustle of life.

The uniqueness of each person is expressed in the external traits and features of the body. For example, it is a well-known fact that no one has the same fingerprint as you or I have, dear reader. The retina, the hand geometry, face shape, the blood system, the DNA, the shape of the earlobe, all have these amazing properties. All these listed features for each person is individual and are unique to them. All these facts speak loudly about one thing: everyone has their own unique make up that only belongs to them, their own exclusive destiny!

Just in the same way as there are no two snowflakes, so also are no two people are alike. Each person is created by God unique:

- *by their appearance*
- *temperament*
- *nature*
- *by their gifts, abilities and talents*

We are all like colored glass in a kaleidoscope, engaged together to make a complete picture of the world. Imagine how our world would be poorer if we leave only pieces of glass of the same color or a certain size and shape? It is the distinctiveness or difference of each individual that makes them indispensable, even in the absence of one individual, a valuable component will be missed. Every human life has certain positive things that another person could not ever provide. We should remember this so we never cease to honor each other's differences, honor the life of every individual.

The most valuable thing in the world is a human being. Why, you ask? First, man is God's creation. Second, because man is the image and likeness of his Creator, is the crown of His creation, the best of all that He created on the earth. God is multifaceted and He created each person in such a way as to reveal Himself in each person in a certain unique way. That is why every person has value.

One very well-known psychologist began his seminar on psychology, holding up a $100 bill. In the hall were about 200 people. The psychologist asked who wants to get a bill. All, as a team, raised their hands.

"Before one of you will receive this bill, I will do something with it", continued the psychologist. He crumpled it and then asked, "does someone still want to get it?" Again, all raised their hands.

Then, he said "I will do the following", throwing the bill on the floor, slightly trampled it with his shoe on the dirty floor. Then he picked up the bill it was wrinkled and dirty.

"Well, to whom of you is this $100 bill still of any use in this form?"

Yet again all raised their hands.

"Dear friends", said the psychologist, "you have just received an illustrative and valuable lesson. In spite of all that I have done with the $100 bill, you all still wanted to get it because it did not lose its value. It is still money, still $100."

In our life, it sometimes happens that we are knocked out of the saddle, trampled, lying in the mud, there at the bottom of life. This can happen to anyone. In such situations, people tend to feel worthless and useless. However, no matter what happens or has happened to you, you will never, under any circumstances, lose your value. Dirty or clean, crumpled or ironed. You will **always** remain invaluable because your value is not determined by what you do, or by whom you are related to but who you originally are. Originally, you are a personality, **endowed** with value.

THE UNIQUENESS OF EACH PERSON IS DETERMINED BY THEIR SPECIFIC MISSION

We are all geniuses.But if you judge a fish by its ability to climb a tree, it will live a lifetime, considering himself a fool.

- Albert Einstein (1879 - 1955), physicist,theorist, Nobel Prize in Physics, public figure,humanist

Imagine this scene: a fish, stubbornly trying to climb a tree. At the foot of the tree has gathered a crowd of curious animals. Some with a look of surprise on their faces, others hooting, following the attempts of the fish to climb to the top of the tree. Funny, Isn't it? We know that fish do not climb trees. Yes, it is not necessary, because the natural habitation and the destiny of fish is water. In swimming, fish are an unbeatable ace. You must admit the fish was not created to climb a tree. Is this a sign of a weak mental ability of fish? Or that its life is worthless and meaningless? Hardly!

The fish looks ridiculous, trying to climb a tree, because it took to running the wrong business. The fish cannot survive outside of the water that God gave it fins, tail and scales for. The fish does not even have lungs to breathe fully while it attempts to climb a tree. The fish

does not have feet and hands to grab a hold of the tree to successfully climb up it. All that is available to it are gills, which are intended for the implementation of respiratory function in water. Question: what does a fish want to do on a tree? How did it get there?

What does this mean for us? It just means that one is better at, let's say, running, the other, long jumping, yet another is well equipped to do something which neither the first nor the second can, they sing so beautifully that you cannot stop listening to them! Perhaps he runs slowly despite their super singing ability. Apparently, to sing fulfills their purpose, they don't need the ability to run fast. Each of these features do not detract from the merits of the others, it does not make one better or worse than others. GIFTS AND ABILITIES OF EVERYONE IS INCOMPARABLE WITH GIFTS AND ABILITIES OF OTHERS.

Michael Bekbok, a former Canadian Hockey player and now coach in the NHL, knowingly states: «in life we need not to strive to overtake others but ourselves." This means that our task is not to compete with other people, "you have overtaken me here but in this thing, I'll surpass you!» If we are busy with these absurd contests, we are wasting our lives, our strength, energy and talent in trying to be better than someone or prove something to someone. There is nothing more foolish than this! Stop comparing yourselves with each other, stop comparing people and hanging labels on them. Stop putting people who has behavior that is totally different from ours into our own framework and standards. Don't be offended by people who are not like us or do not come in line with our expectations. The reason why it's not worth doing is that each of us have our own specificity and individuality dictated by the mission that we have to fulfill.

CAN YOU SEE A «STAR» IN THE OTHER PERSON?

If a person can see a «star» in the other person, then they will never suffer from depression, they will never have bad emotions, never have a bad day. Everyone you see will bring you joy and you will do the same for them, you will be genuinely happy for them and they will enrich your life. Imagine this: a person constantly observes other people, making them compliments, happy for them. What do you think? will such a person be on the verge of depression? Never in life! They simply have no time to be depressed. Depression arise from a person ceasing to notice «stars» in others, to be happy for them and honor them. For someone that does notice others, every person they meet will be the reward that enriches his life.

EACH «STAR» YOU NOTICE, ILLUMINATES YOUR LIFE. Each «star» you notice, gives light, even if you do not always notice. Remember, when there is total darkness, even the light of «stars» can be life-saving. Each «star» that you notice has something that can enrich you. From each person that you give compliments, you notice something good, you get even more than what they can give you. Each «star» we notice enriches and illuminates our lives. When you notice people: their uniqueness, their character, their beauty, it will bring you more dividends, because «It is more blessed to give than to receive.»

When there is no wisdom, a person does not see differences. Even if they see differences, they do not see «stars» in them. This is because the only «star» they see is them self! With this kind of attitude people are driving themselves into depression. **IF THE ONLY «STAR» A PERSON SEES IS THEM SELF, YOUR EYES HAVE NO PLACE OF REST, NO PLACE TO STOP AND EXPLORE, NO PLACE TO HAVE FUN, SUCH A PERSON WILL FALL INTO DEPRESSION.** This means that they lack wisdom, are too full of them self, to make room for someone else. When a person is too obsessed with them self, he loses wisdom.

- When you are too obsessed with yourself, you lose the gift of wisdom

- When you are too obsessed with yourself, you become stupid

Anyone who we emphasize, every person whose difference we recognize, every time we appreciate people and emphasize what is special about them, it brings us a profit. The wealth they possess, becomes ours. You want evidence?

You honored someone and then that person gives you a job

You honored someone and then they become your customer

You honored someone and through that person you entered into completely new possibilities

The «Star», you noticed, then becomes the source of your enlightenment and illumination.

IT IS NOT ENOUGH TO RECOGNIZE THE «STAR» IN THE OTHER PERSON

It is not enough to recognize the "star» in another person, there is a need to honor this person, by giving something to let them know that you have discerned their difference.

Honor - the ability to sacrifice and pay the price, to prove to another person that they are special. When a wise person discerns a "star" in a person, they take gifts and hit the road to honor this person. It is not enough to RECOGNIZE the "star» in other people, we must have a desire to do something for them, give something to them, to pay the price, to make the person know that you honor them for their special features.

You know what some of us do? They say, «I honor that person in my heart!» and they do not even know. If you respect a person somewhere deep in your heart, no one will know about it. **Honor is different from respect.** Did you ever respect a person and they did not even know that you related to them this way? We note something special in people, but rarely tell them about it. Sometimes we think, « I admire this person, I love them, they are very precious to me» but the question is: Do they know about it? Does the person know how good you feel about them? Are all the people around you aware of how highly you regard them? If not, then you did not tell them about it, you did not tell them compliments, you did not mark the differences of others enough. God forbid something happens to them before you tell them how you feel, you will regret it for the rest of your life. Make a decision: «I will make a list of all, the good things in my husband or wife, in the people around me and I will tell them. I will not keep quiet about the positive traits, those positive things that I see in my family, friends and acquaintances. I will emphasize the fact that they are good, so they know for what I am honoring them.»

When we are silent, the «star» of the other people cannot shine around us. When we are silent, we live in our problems, and they are driving us into a corner, into the darkness, making us to live only for ourselves, when we are supposed to live not only for ourselves but also for the people around us. I appeal to the men: maybe you do not understand your wife but you do not need to understand her, she must be honored! Maybe she's not like you, yes, that is her difference, that's why God brought you together. You must say out loud those things for which you honor, celebrate and value her, for what you are grateful to her.

Let us ask forgiveness for disregard, ingratitude, being rude to each other, for dishonor towards husband or wife, children, friends, acquaintances, to all people we are surrounded by. Let's practice respect towards those in whom we discern difference, in whom we recognize a «star". Let's sacrifice, give up something for these people. This is especially important if there is something you do not like, something that irritates you in the other person. That's when you need to give him, a precious gift to kill the hate in you, so you do not become another Cain. (Learn more about who is Cain, see Chapter 7).

For something to enrich your life, you need to learn recognize and honor it. You must COMMEMORATE THE «STAR» IN THE OTHER PERSON SO THEY CAN ENRICH YOU. What you fail to recognize and honor, will never be able to enrich you. All that we ignore, everything that we do not recognize, all that we do not honor, we lose. Where we refuse to honor, to make compliments, we lose. Where we do not recognize and honor, we not only do not gain but also lose.

You know, dear friends, you also are not recognized enough. Do you know why, you can be in a bad mood? Because you are not hearing what you are supposed to hear, no one celebrates you, your difference is insufficiently emphasized by those around you. Let's change this!

WHAT SHOULD BE OUR REACTION TO A «STAR»?

If we are not used to making compliments to people from time to time then the «stars» of other people may inadvertently overshadow us and even dazzle us with its light and this can cause irritation. In general, if we are not careful, alien «stars» may irritate us because at this moment they are:

- Better
- brighter or
- at the moment, you are not a «star» in the given area or sphere

At the same time, it is important to remember: NOTING THE «STAR» OF ANOTHER PERSON DOES NOT MEAN TO EXCHANGE YOUR OWN «STAR», not at all! It's a mistake to think that if you raise someone else, honor someone else's «star», then yours will fade. To regard someone else's «star» means, on the contrary, to strengthen their light, because thanks to reflected light, as in a mirror, your «star» starts to shine even brighter.

A «star» is that which is a little better than you, because you're not a star, just an ordinary person. Maybe you too are a «star», but that «star» was slightly brighter than the other «stars», maybe a little bit more glorious than other "stars" and it is some else's fame, someone else, not you, the underlining of someone else's virtues but not yours, that can vex us. Therefore, we must be extremely careful and watch what state our heart is.

It is important to remember that recognizing the «stars» in ANOTHER PERSON DOES NOT imply to kill or put off your own «star», not at all! It is an error to think that if you raise the other person, honoring another «star», yours will fade. On the contrary, to celebrate another «star» means to strengthen your own light because thanks to the reflection of light as in a mirror, your «star» shines even brighter.

Even if you do not immediately see a «star» in others, look for them, I beg you! Because sometimes we do not notice something nice in others, we are used to seeing in them something negative, because it is more evident. We must understand one very important thing: each person has a «star.» Someone is endowed with five talents, his «star» is greater. Another has two, his «star» is smaller. Somebody has just one but this does not negate the principle that every person is a «star.» **Wisdom is eager to see, to learn and recognize the «star» in others.**

Dear reader, let us learn to notice the «star» in other people and not just see our own «star». When you open the «stars» in others, they begin to build you up and illuminate you. Only the «star» that we see, shares with us their light. That «star» that we do not notice, does not give us their light and when the sky has no stars then everywhere is complete darkness. When we see even a small star in the night sky, they enlighten and illuminate us.

To learn more about this topic I recommend that you read the book «Who am I?".

Chapter Summary

1. **When we see people, and emphasize their features, it brings us a profit.** The wealth they possess, becomes ours.

2. **It is important to not only notice people, but to learn how to read their differences.** Only when sacrifice and dedication is required from us do we truly honor the gifts of another person.

3. **To be silent when you see something extraordinary means to try to eclipse the light of someone's «star", to put it off, to ignore it.** This is equivalent to murder.

In summing up this chapter, I want to stress that we have laid emphasis on the fact that everybody is a «star.» We discussed the issues of the uniqueness and diversity of each person. In the next chapter, we will look in details at what happens when we do not understand the law ofdifference. In it we will look at the following questions.

- What could be worse than to go crazy?

- Who is Cain?

- When we do not understand the law differences, we live on the imposed societal patterns and stereotypes

- Harm of generalizations

- When we do not understand the law difference, we are indifferent to what is happening

GOLDEN TRUTHS

A unique combination of external and internal qualities of a person, as a whole is wealth

Everyone is a treasure

Each person has a destiny, unique and inherent only to them

Each "star» that you notice illuminates your life

If the only «star» you see is yourself, then your eyes have no place of rest, no place to stop and explore, no place to have fun, therefore such a person falls into depression

It is not enough to recognize a "star « in a person, we need to honor the person, sacrifice something to let them know that you have noted their difference

We must celebrate the "star" in a person to be enriched by them

If we are not careful, the alien «stars» may irritate us

A «star» is that which is slightly better than you, because you're not a star, you're just an ordinary person

To celebrate the «star» in another person does not mean to put off your own «star»

SELF – ASSESSMENT

1. Do you agree with the fact that each person is unique and therefore has a specific and unique destiny?

    1) No (0)

    2) Yes (1)

2. With whom do you compete?

    1) With others (0)

    2) With you (1)

3. Are you pleased and happy meeting other people?

    1) No (0)

    2) Yes (1)

4. How often do you tell people close to you, what you see in them that makes you happy?

    1) Rarely, almost never (0)

    2) Often (1)

EVALUATION OF TEST RESULTS

(0 points) We're sorry, you find it hard to notice advantages and to honor the «stars» in others. You are irritated by the light of alien «stars». You are too obsessed by yourself, you are the only «star» which you tend to notice on the horizon of your life. Remember: all that we ignore, everything that we do not recognize, all that we do not honor, we lose. You can remain lonely, trying to escape from all the «stars» that appear in your way. However, good news! Continue reading the book, and then you can avoid such losses in your life.

(1 - 3 points) Not bad! you have a desire to recognize the «stars» in others. However, even when you see something unusual and surprising in others, something worth admiration and praise, you prefer to keep quiet and keep it to yourself. The reason for this is not humility, rather a lack of understanding of the law of difference. Begin honoring differences of other people and your life will become much richer and more colorful. Further reading of this book will open your eyes even more to many of your questions.

(4 points) Congratulations! You are aware of the value and uniqueness of each individual, you are ready to honor the «star» in each. It does not infringe upon or deprive you of your self-confidence. It implies that you have a healthy self-esteem and the right attitude towards people around you. Such wealth cannot be left lying like an untouched load. Share your positive attitude of life with your friends and family, shine!

GUIDELINES FOR THE IMPLEMENTATION OF PRACTICAL TASKS

1.   CAUTION: These activities should not only be read and forgotten, they are VERY IMPORTANT. According to many years of working with people I know people often perform such tasks «for the sake of it" but it's your life, this is for you, take them seriously.

2. To maximize results, I suggest performing the tasks within the 24 hours, otherwise, you will forget, get distracted and you will distance yourself from the results you want.

3. To answer all the questions, find a quiet place and systematically work out the tasks.

4. Meditate on each chapter, on all the points that you underlined for yourself, reflect on the them and write out your steps of action.

5. Set yourself a time frame, constraints, to help you not to put off working on yourself.

6. Find someone you can be accountable to, who could help remind you to stay focused on working on yourself.

PRACTICAL TASKS

Examine your life and answer these questions.

Do you notice the difference in other people?

Do you recognize the differences in each person you meet on your life's journey?

Do you protect the differences of other people?

Do you give freedom to the differences of others?

Do you help the differences of other people to flourish?

Can you celebrate the «star» in others?

How do you respond to people who are greater champions, more vivid than yourself?

Are you able to feel safe and comfortable in the presence of the glory of others?

Make a list of all the good that is in your spouse and in the people around you, and begin to tell them about it. Do not be silent about the positive traits, of those positive things that you notice in your friends and acquaintances. Emphasize what is good in them, make them aware so that they know that they have something they can be celebrated and honored for.

Tasks to perform in a group of (very nice for a husband and a wife to perform this exercise together). Look at your partner, without asking too many questions, discover and recognize five things in this person that makes them special, for which you can be thankful. Honestly tell your partner what you can learn from them.

Having discovered the differences in others, it is necessary to sacrifice, to honor those differences. Prepare a gift for your partner with whom you are engaged in this exercise. This is especially necessary if the person has something you don't really like. That's when you have to give them something so highly valuable enough to kill the hate in yourself.

CHAPTER 7

WHEN WE DO NOT UNDERSTAND THE LAW OF DIFFERENCE

WHEN WE DO NOT UNDERSTAND THE LAW OF DIFFERENCE

You cannot humiliate a person,
and not be humiliated with him.

- Booker T. Washington (1856 - 1915),
outstanding fighter for the education
of black Americans, orator, politician, writer

In the previous chapter the fact that every person is a «star" was widely covered. We talked about the uniqueness and diversity of each person. In this chapter, we'll talk about what happens when people do not understand the law of differences. **When we do not understand the law of differences, sometimes we cause irreparable damage to people, and at the same time ourselves.** We hurt, humiliate and literally kill people, if not physically, then morally. Booker Taliaferro Washington, one of the most outstanding educators, the statement of whom I gave as an epigraph to this chapter, rightly noted the relationship between the person who is humiliated and the one humiliating him.

After the act of humiliation, both become links of the same chain. If you allow yourself to insult people, remember: in the same way you humiliate yourself, you are inseparably connected with your victim. Although we humiliate other people to somehow, some way, fend off, get rid of the one who became the object of humiliation. Not understanding the law of difference, we will pierce souls and create in them a gaping wound, formless holes, that fester and stink, causing suffering to a living person. Sometimes such painful wounds are difficult to heal. The lack of understanding of the law of difference leads to serious consequences.

WHAT COULD BE WORSE THAN TO GO CRAZY?

Success: the only unforgivable sin in relation to your loved ones.

- Faina Ranevskaya (1896 - 1984), the Soviet theater and film actress

Let's look at another historical story: the story of Cain and Abel.

Who are Cain and Abel? These are two Biblical characters, the two sons of Adam and Eve, who lived on Earth at the dawn of humanity. Abel was a rancher, and his brother Cain, a farmer. Conflicts between them occurred because of sacrifice to God. When Abel sacrificed animals the firstborn of his flock, God graciously accepted his sacrifice. Cain also as sacrifice, brought fruits of the earth, but they were rejected by God. Cain saw that God gave preference to the sacrifice of Abel, became angry and did not find anything better to do than to kill his brother. When God asked, «Where is Abel your brother?", he replied «am I my brother's keeper?» Since then the name of Cain has become synonymous with evil and is used to refer to a malicious, envious man capable of any level of hate against even the closest people to them.

So, do you know, dear reader, why Cain killed Abel? He did it because he did not understand the law differences, and because:

Cain could not honor the distinction of Abel
He could not honor and celebrate the victory of his brother,
He could not celebrate the differences, he decided to get rid of his brother, to kill him.

THERE ARE TWO CATEGORIES OF PEOPLE WHO DO NOT SEE DIFFERENCES. The first category of people who do not see difference, do it because they live **only for their problems,** which leads them to depression and then on the bed of a psychiatric hospital! However, there is another category of people who are worse than those who do not see the difference and do not utter any compliments to others as a reason of utter focus on their own affairs and problems. So, what could be worse than madness? If you think that there is nothing worse than, to go crazy, you're wrong! **The most terrible thing is when you recognize the difference in a person and you become ill because he or she is better than you.** The most terrible thing is when you see this person's difference and you become sad that

he is more well-groomed than you, more beautiful than you. So, you summon all efforts to skip this moment and ignore the fact that, for example, the girl has a new hairstyle even though she is your best friend. Her new dress is more impressive than yours, in the real sense you saw it, but pretend as if you did not and immediately redirect the course of the conversation to talk about other things: "how are things at work? « Now is not the time to talk about work! This is the time to emphasize to your friend about her new beautiful dress: first make a compliment and then talk about work. Your friend is here now, you can come back to talk about work. First take note of what should be taken note of!

You know what this is called? Very simply: «nothing grieves people as the happiness of their neighbors! NOTHING PLEASES PEOPLE AS THE GRIEF OF THEIR NEIGHBORS!» Translated into our everyday language it means: "she has a new dress, then I have depression; She has failed at work, I have reason to breathe a sigh of relief and rejoice, saying that not only do I have everything bad, someone else is also not lucky, isn't this a good reason to rejoice?" This is the reason we don't make compliments and do not notice the good in people. We feel it is better not to notice, just pretend that you don't, that you "missed it", rather than summon the strength to find the positives, the good qualities of a person and say it out loud. People, are you still here? I think it won't do us any harm to think about these things?

It is one thing not to notice the difference, but then when you see them and do not say it out loud, it is wickedness. With time, we will react especially when other people have started to talk about it, have noticed the difference, then we have nowhere to hide, it becomes difficult to pretend you still don't see anything, then we have to admit: «Yes, yes, you look good!», but this is not good!

This last option, believe me, is worse than just going mad. If I get sick because someone has all going well or someone has things going great, it means that my behavior has traces of Cain. What did Cain do? Unlike those of us who at point blank do not see the differences of others, Cain saw the differences in his brother Abel. The problem is that sometimes the differences of others irritate us. This was the problem of Cain, he became jealous of this difference, and this envy led him to kill his brother. Envy haunted Cain and gave him no peace until he decided to get rid of the source of his ill health, which deprived him of rest. He decided that it was easier to kill Abel, eliminating the irritant factor out of his life, rather than put up with his differences, those extraordinary abilities that enabled his brother to succeed more than himself.

Faina Georgievna Ranevskaya said remarkably, «success is the only unforgivable sin towards our close relatives». Very often, we cannot forgive our family that they have succeeded in something more than us. Have you ever caught yourself thinking that you hold this unforgiveness against your family in you? **If you look at some** differences in people, at someone's successes and you do not want to rejoice with them, moreover, you feel bad because someone is successful and you are jealous then, however sad it might be to me, I have to inform you, dear reader, you are like Cain, a murderer of your own brother! If you do not overcome and get rid of this jealousy, then sooner or later it will lead you to murder. You know, we can kill people not only physically but also morally, emotionally, with words and attitude.

What does it mean to «kill» a person? All that needs to be said is, «*Shut up! Who are you? You are nobody!*». With these words, we can crush and kill people, it is the same as fratricide (brother killing). If we give a person the feeling that they are not appreciated, that they are not worthy, we have destroyed them, this is the same as murder. Even the desire to destroy the person mentally and emotionally, that they «vanish out of sight, out of mind» means that you want to bring about their nonexistence, thus you have killed them! Maybe in your own opinion you "have done well" and have gotten even with your enemies. You must remember one very important thing: one who kills, reaps IN THEIR LIFE the same. Another person will come along and just like you have done, will smash you against a wall.

That's why we need to be careful in relationships between husbands and wives. Some husbands forcefully assert their authority over their wives and begin to humiliate them, to mentally crush their identity. These husbands are not husbands at all, I tell you, these husbands are killers! Husbands are called to be a fortress for their wives, to create an atmosphere in the home, where his wife and children feel complete security and comfort around him. If a man wants to create comfort in the house and the wife is a threat to his plans, he is ready to destroy her, just to secure his peace. Then you are not a man, you are a killer! Here's what can be worse than madness in life: the way Cain behaved in killing his own brother. It all starts with the fact that we refuse to notice and honor the differences of others, to see their difference as a source of our exaltation and not the source of our defeat.

WHO IS CAIN?

- **Cain is a person who is not prepared to honor and celebrate the differences of other people**

- **Cain is the one who was not able to rightly evaluate the differences in others, decided to ignore a person, to kill them morally, to destroy them**

- **Cain is the one who refuses to protect the one who is different from him**

Do you know what this is called? **When you do not celebrate a person, who is in one way or the other better than you, it is a manifestation of the behavior of Cain, which can end in murder.** First you do not recognize and «close your eyes" to their achievements and benefits, then it will begin to haunt you from the inside and then turn

into envy. If you do not notice right away the benefits of the person, then it generates envy, which in turn ends finally in murder and this does not necessarily mean physically removing the person.

What does murder mean? It is to say for example: «*She's nothing, I'm better than her! Yes, she is married well, although I'm not married I am more intelligent, better looking, I'm still more beautiful. If she has done something good in life, it is only because she was lucky.*» Such a person agrees to the course of this thoughts in his head. This hidden desire to destroy a person is sure to find its expression in words like, «You are nobody! You are not worth anything! « With these words, you have killed a person. This is murder when you destroy a man morally, when you humiliate a person, deprive them of their dignity, make them feel last among people, like nobody of significance. If you want to get rid of a person you delete him from your life, in this way you've killed him! So often do superiors behave with their subordinates, destroying them morally. This is a «Cain» mentality and action and smells like fratricide again. Don't do this! If a person has a difference, mark them, underline their differences and celebrate this person.

Reading about the relationship between Cain and Abel, we must pay attention to the next details. Asked where his brother Abel was, Cain answered, with cold detachment: «am I my brother's keeper?» He showed that he has removed from himself any responsibility for what is happening, happened or will happen to the closest person, who was in his life at the time, his own brother. Cain not only refused to see the differences in Abel, honor them, but he wanted to get rid of his brother, so much so, that he did not care where he was, or to delve a little into the twists and turns of his life. What does it mean to «become his brother's keeper?" To support people, to defend their differences. **You must understand that «becoming your brother's keeper» means not only be able to see, celebrate and honor the differences of those around us, but also to cover their back in difficult moments, show empathy, support and participate in their lives.**

Therefore, dear reader, let's stop behaving like Cain, who was so blinded by envy, so much that he did not stop at raising his hand against the closest person to him, his own brother by blood. Let's not be those who destroy the difference and dignity of other people, but those who protect them, who literally become in the true meaning of the word, "keepers of their brothers" those who provide support and assistance to all who need it.

If after reading the story of Cain, you conclude that he is a bad person, then know that you have judged yourself! Each of us has been Cain at some stage in our lives. We are all like Cain. Perhaps we do not kill people physically, but each of us know how we behave when we see that someone is different from us. If you are more or less «good-mannered «, then at best you ignore and do not notice the person just because he is different: «He is not here, I do not see anybody even at close range!» How does this correspond to reality?

THE PROBLEM IS THAT CAIN LIVES IN EACH OF US. In each of us there is jealousy, there is a desire to compete. If we do not fight with ourselves, with our weaknesses, we will not even notice when we reduce to fratricide. At what stages of our life, do we all behave like Cain. **We begin to behave like Cain, when seeing a person who is different from us, we in the best instance, ignore them, in the worst scenario we seek to «kill» them.** We need to resist the action of this Spirit. Husbands do not delete the «star» in your wives! Do not destroy the woman! Let her shine, let her blossom, be a defender of women, not her oppressor. We need to know how to honor people who are different from us. We need to know how to celebrate, to encourage, to build up, lift up, people who do not belong to your camp, but are part of another group.

Has it happened that you noticed something special in a person: beautiful face, nice hair, tasteful clothes and kept silent? Know that this is the beginning of Cain. **NEVER REMAIN SILENT WHEN YOU SEE THAT SOMEONE HAS ACHIEVED GREAT SUCCESS!** Be sure to celebrate it somehow, at least say a good word. Do not be silent! Your reaction, your silence says more about you than a mass of words. This means that you are not happy with the success of a person, you will not be able to celebrate them. If you continue in that habit you will only feel sick when you see the good in others. ALL GOOD THINGS THAT WE SEE IN PEOPLE WE MUST APPRECIATE AND SAY IT OUT LOUD.

One should always notice what differentiates people and compliment them. The wise notes differences in whatever way it is expressed. Even if a person looks bad, appreciate them, don't be misled by the signals that his unpresentable appearance sends. Maybe it is in your power to provide help to them, maybe you can express your sympathy to them, perhaps they need your participation in their life today. Just your smile alone could change his life. Think about it!

Whatever the difference - good or bad - notice and NEVER be silent! Silence this is the worst type of response. Being silent is the worst thing you can do in any situation, whether good or evil. We must always respond to both good and evil. There is a wonderful parable that illustrates well the importance of the choices we make in life.

Once upon a time - an old Indian revealed to his grandson an important life truth,

- In every man there is a struggle, much like the struggle between two wolves. One wolf represents evil - envy, jealousy, regret, ambition, lies...

The other wolf represents good, love, hope, truth, goodness, faithfulness...

The Little Indian, touched by the words of his grandfather, thought for a moment and then asked:

- And which wolf wins at the end?

The Old Indian smiled slightly and replied:

- The wolf you feed always wins.

If we make a choice in favor of good, the world in general gains, in it increases the «content» of good and evil does not exceed the critical mass. If we make a choice in favor of evil, then it begins to exponentially multiply and the muddy wave of evil catches and covers us. If we do not win over Cain in us, it will affect us all together, ourselves, and the people around us. People will be encouraged to do evil to themselves and the people around them, bringing suffering, pain and destruction. If Cain in our soul is defeated, we will become a beacon of light in this complex world that is desperately choking from lack of love, hope and forgiveness.

WHEN WE DO NOT UNDERSTAND THE LAW OF DIFFERENCE, WE LIVE BY IMPOSED SOCIAL NORMS AND STEREOTYPES

When we do not understand the law of difference each of us individually and collectively are not ready to receive people who are not like the rest. Although everyone is proud and literally brags that they are an individual, different, not like everybody else around, original, does not want to copy anyone, yet everyone knows how and how not to behave themselves based on how others behave. There are many behavioral patterns in our society, according to which all the inhabitants of our country know what is accepted and what is not accepted. These unwritten rules are a kind of restrictions for people, to which they adapt their daily lives, they are called 'social norms' and 'stereotypes'.

We all know that men do not cry, they do not need to show any feelings, they must be tough or he is not considered a «real man.» If you are a girl, you are programmed from childhood to get married and have children. After all, the misconception is that a «woman's happiness lies strictly in having a good man close by". It is so prevalent that if you are single and on your own, then you are a strange woman, being content on your own does not fit the social norms or stereotype. According to social norms, the ideal woman should also be 'blonde with blue eyes, no extra weight, with high breasts and long legs'. Unfortunately, only a Barbie doll can fit this ideal exactly. All the same this mind-set is driving millions of women into depression and pushing them into dangerous experiments to change their own body shape and appearance. It impacts the psyche of many women negatively.

For example, everyone knows how to behave in public transport. We all agree that we should not talk loud in a public transport, if you have entered a bus, train or subway, you need to sit down or stand up and mind your own business, look anywhere but not at the people, don't talk loudly. This is considered the norm in society. When foreigners appear on the bus, acting free, out of control and noisy it is considered bad manners and we forgive them because they are foreigners, not knowing the norms. These norms force us to condemn such behavior we are confident that those foreigners in the public transport who demonstrate freedom are bad mannered, not normal, not for once hesitating to think, maybe we are not normal. We,

who for some reason have inherited these norms and are religiously following them.

There are also norms about how to behave in public and public facilities. People understand what is expected of them and what is accepted in society, how to behave according to conventional expectations and norms. We find it hard to engage in conversation with a stranger on the street, or greet someone. Sometimes on the streets it will cause confusion and even fear, they would say "what do you want from me?" We somehow tend to think that on the streets only people who are trying to sell things or members of religious sects can approach us, contact with whom could be dangerous since they can influence our subconscious. According to some unwritten and unspoken directives it is assumed that a normal person would not seek an occasion to get acquainted with, smile or greet you if you are not familiar with them. This is weird, Isn't it?

When we do not understand the law of difference we do not think that someone may behave differently than people in our surrounding. We do not give people the freedom of expression and restrict ourselves to this framework and stereotypes. We do not allow people to be different from us and look with suspicion at those, who do not behave «as accepted» while "just as accepted" are those stereotypes and norms imposed on us by unknown and timeless sources. The law of difference is the law of freedom, welcoming the differences of people in all manifestations!

In the family, there are also established norms. For example, we divide household duties by those which 'apply to men' and those that do not apply. Women, by default, must be able to do everything and do it expeditiously because as they say, the «home is the place of woman,» her mission - «keep the family home». The culture of honor is not incorporated in the upbringing of our children, so it has become the norm to build relationships between parents and children very democratically: if a child does not agree with the demands of the parents, they act up in public, arguing with their parents, claiming independence, after all they say, "I am a personality, my own man (or woman), I can do what I want" and "who are my parents anyway?" they feel they are only people who are called to give them «a happy childhood.»

If we do not discern which people are valuable to us, none more valuable than our parents, they are the ones we must honor unconditionally, then we lose there, where we are supposed to gain. Not understanding the law of difference and living according to the established stereotypes in our society, we stop seeing the value of categories of people in our lives and create problems for ourselves. Behaving according to these established norms, can impact in an unacceptable way to those who are worthy of an entirely different attitude on our part. We insult and we lose the most precious people to us, relatives and friends.

THE HARM OF GENERALIZATIONS

You laugh at me because I am different from you, and I laugh at you because you are not different from each other.

- Mikhail Bulgakov (1891 - 1940),
Russian writer, playwright, theater director and actor

What is the usual reaction of people to those who are not like them? Mikhail Bulgakov, author of novels and short stories, dozens of humorous anecdotes, plays, dramatizations, screenplays and librettos, argues that it is laughter. For the most part we scoff at those who are different to us. Differences scare and repel us, we strive to defuse them by any means, run from them, and "the dangerous troublemakers", who dare to be different, we pronounce the sentence: death - physical or moral. Must it be this way? [12]

As seen from the above examples, established generalizations, norms and stereotypes are harmful to mutual understanding. As part of popular culture, they form a niche, in which it is easy to judge the behavior of different people, evaluate them and on this basis, we easily form our attitude to one or the other category of people. For example: «all men want from women is only one

---

[12] *Offset - to destroy, to smooth differences between someone - or something - else*

thing», «all Asians look the same», «all Jews are stingy», «people from the village have very low ethics and low level of development". **Norms and stereotypes are nothing but an attempt to place a mark on a person or group of people based on only some characteristics.** It is an attempt to «categorize» people. Anyone who violates these unspoken standards and unwritten truth, become subject to attack, suspicions, etc.

Journalist Walter Lippmann in his book «Public Opinion», published in 1922, highlights four aspects of stereotypes.

1. **Stereotypes simplify reality:** thanks to them, complex characteristics of a person or group of people are formulated with the help of two or three sentences.

2. **People are more likely to borrow from the stereotypes of their friends, the media and so on.** Rather than formulating them based on their own life experiences.

3. **Almost all stereotypes are false,** they almost always attribute to a specific person, traits that they are obliged to have only as a result of belonging to a particular group.

4. **Stereotypes die hard:** even if people understand that their beliefs are not true, they tend to not reject them, and argue that those are just exceptions that proves the rule. [16]

Generalizations are harmful because thanks to them, a complex and diverse world becomes conventional and stereotyped. All that we fix in the form of rigid stereotypes, deprive us of the possibility of change. If we categorize a person into the group of, «whiners» or «losers» or "strange", it is very difficult to observe some changes, although such a person has long since changed for the better. For this reason, generalizations take restrictive character. If once a person has failed, made a mistake or was publicly disgraced, then a label is firmly glued to them, which not only people believe, but also the person will start to act within the framework of the «settled» opinion. They become what people say they are. After that they are often afraid to go beyond the «permitted» concept, their life becomes a confirmation of public opinion, which was formed about this person. As the saying goes: «If a man would be called a pig for a long time, soon he will grunt like a pig». That is, getting into a rut of some successfully formed a cliché, a person becomes controlled by those claims. For example, if a child is not quite smart, usually ignorant parents or teachers put the label «stupid» on the child after which the child begins to «justify» the expectations of the adults. [13]

One of the most common misconceptions is to categorize people as good, evil, stupid, smart. A man has freedom of movement, and has many possibilities: he was foolish – but became smart, was evil – but became good and vice versa. This is the greatness of man and so

---

[13] *Cliche - Template expressions used to to in short, form to classify and evaluate entities or phenomena.*

you should not judge a person. "You condemn them, but meanwhile they have already changed for the better» This wise statement belongs to Leo Tolstoy (1828 - 1910), one of the Russian writers and revered by many one of the greatest writers of the world. Tolstoy was right: thinking according to stereotypes and trying to put people into a Procrustean bed of our established and stagnated opinions, we ourselves fall into a trap. A person has long qualitatively changed, yet we continue to look at them through the lens of patterns and stereotypes firmly entrenched in our minds. Or worse still: we ourselves have long been due to change, cast off for example, the patterns of behavior of our society, imposed on us through education and transmitted at the genetic level by our parents and grandparents. Instead we, with the tenacity of a bear continue to live on the patch of space that was once measured out for us. [14]

Once upon a time in a small provincial town, polar explorers got a white polar bear as a gift. To keep the bear a large cage with a pool was needed, so the bear was placed temporarily in the biggest cage that could be found in the zoo. Even this cage was too tight for the white giant. Poor Bear all day pacing the cage: four steps to one side, heavily turning around, brushing the cage with his sides, then four steps into another turn again...

---

[14] *Procrustean bed, in the bed, on the robber Procrustes force was putting travelers: обрубал part of the body that does not fit, little stretched body (the name of Procrustes - «stretching»). in a figurative sense - that does not meet the essence of the phenomenon. Expression «Procrustean bed» means that the desire to or under the rigid framework or artificial yardstick, sometimes sacrificing anything - anything substantial.*

After a while next to the bear cage was a swimming pool and a fence. The bars of the old cell were dismantled and the bear was in a new spacious enclosure. But the bear continued to stroll the old way: four steps to one side, four steps to another... During the time that he was in a small cage, he built a solid cage within himself. During this time, the cell grew into him and became part of him.

Our limiting beliefs, patterns and stereotypes eats into our identity so that we no longer notice them and think that it is we ourselves who think that way. We do not even think why we behave this way. Certain actions, reactions and behaviors become our nature, so that we are not even aware of them.

To look at all the people around through the prism of patterns as if in none of them is something special, does not require special Intelligence. Even unintelligent people are capable of this. To ignore others and not even try to notice their differences, does not require great mental abilities. **To see the differences, note the special features, discover what is remarkable in a person, one must work hard, that is solve a task of enormous complexity, for to do this you must seek, look deep, dig deep.** People do not like to work hard mentally, especially where there is no clear benefit for them. The reason for such an attitude is simple, one must summon a lot of strength to see how a person is different from us. We do not want to stretch ourselves.

Back to the words of Mikhail Bulgakov: «you laugh at me because I am different from you, and I laugh at you because you are not different from each other.» At first glance, the author of this quote deserved pity, because he was subjected to ridicule by those who discovered that he was different from them. But in reality, it is not those who are different that should be pitied, but those who do not come out of the accepted stereotypes, those who do not differ from the crowd. Worthy of regret are those who look at the world through the prism of stereotypes and generalized conclusions, trying to place all people into a category, that is **«to relate to different persons equally, without taking into consideration the difference between them»** (the big phrasebook of Michelson). As we will see throughout this book, these things are unacceptable in a healthy community.

WHEN WE DO NOT UNDERSTAND THE LAW DIFFERENCE, WE ARE INDIFFERENT TO WHAT IS HAPPENING

If you are indifferent to the suffering of others, you do not deserve to bear the title Human.

- Saadi (approx. 1881 - 1291),
Persian and Tajik poet, moralist, a practical Sufis

Increasingly, in our social life the concept of «social experiment is more and more becoming a reality.» The main objective of social experiments are to examine our society on important human qualities without which, in fact, our world would not exist. Some enterprising people decided to conduct a simple experiment.

Two children of different nationalities, holding the same plate with a message about their material need, stood in one of the most crowded places of a capital city. How would you react if you saw a person with such a sign? How you react will depend on who that person is by nationality.

The results were shocking: a young man with a clearly «non - Russian» appearance in 2 hours collected only 438 rubles, the other with an obvious Russian face in 1 ½ hours collected 4000 rubles. An elderly woman willingly stretched her hands to the guy with a Slavic appearance, with a large bill of 1000 rubles. Even the homeless, living on the street were not indifferent to this happening on the street. With all her belongings, a homeless woman went to enquire from two guys what was wrong. Although the woman could not help, she suggested an address where the young men, quite possibly could get help. A man, who was old enough to be a father to one of the participants of this experiment, wanted to know what happened, why one of the guys was on the street begging, then not only gave the necessary amount for a ticket - 2000 rubles - but also left his phone number, saying, call me when you get back home. [18]

It turned out that in a country where most of the population is not pure Russian, they related to people with prejudice of other nationalities. It remains only to puzzle, is this racism or deeply rooted stereotypes? Yeah, maybe foreigners from neighboring countries spoiled their reputation but naturally, it can be assumed that in every nation there are both good people and bad. You cannot cut one size to fit all. The conclusion that arises is this: it does not matter who you are, each of us needs to get rid of indifference. We should be a little kinder and respond to the call for help. It's not in the money, but in the human sympathy and compassion.

In Germany, after Hitler came to power, one priest said:

When the Nazis came for the communists, I remained silent. I was not a communist.
When they imprisoned the Social - Democrats, I said nothing. I was not a Social - Democrat.
When they came for the union members, I did not protest. I was not a trade unionist.
When they came for the Jews, I did not revolt. I was not a Jew.
When they came for me, there was no one left who would have stood up for me.

These words of Friedrich Gustav Martin Emil Niemöller (1902-1984), a Protestant theologian, pastor of protestant-evangelic Church, one of the most popular oppositionist to Nazism in Germany, President of the world council of Churches, told us a lot of things, especially this: **we should not remain indifferent to what is happening around us.** If evil is happening around us, we should to talk about it. We can't remain silent in- regards-to evil, as well as in relation to the good, we must not remain indifferent. When you remain silent you are just as guilty as the person committing the offense.

Anton Chekhov (1904), Russian writer, a recognized classic of world literature, a physician by profession, honorable academician of the imperators academy of science, very elegant speaker, one of the most popular dramatists of the world said, "Indifference, this is the paralysis of the soul, a premature death».

Bruno Jasieński (1901 - 1938), a wonderful Polish and Russian writer, who was shot in the 1938, in his novel wrote very true words: "do not be afraid of your friends, at worst they can betray you, do not be afraid of your enemies, at worst they can kill you, be afraid of indifferent people, only with their silent approval, betrayal and murder happens on the earth." The worst enemy of the human soul, which can be is indifference. When we are silent, when we do not react properly to the differences of others, we allow evil to flourish, betrayal and murder. When we do not encourage differences and uniqueness of each inhabitant of the world, we deprive our lives of paints and colors, this generates mediocrity, discouragement and depression, boredom, from which we also suffer.

THERE IS NOTHING MORE TERRIBLE THAN THE WORDS «I DON'T CARE." Ivan Okhlobystin (b. in 1966), Russian actor, director, screenwriter, playwright, journalist, author, wrote a wonderful line on this phenomenon.

Never say « I don't care."

Do not seek to advertise your indifference. *This is not an indication of your independence. Indifference – is a paralysis of the soul.*

What do you feel when you say, «I do not care?»

It becomes empty and cold inside. You are uncomfortable and protest.

Most often, inside yourself, because your neighbor is indifferent….,

Only the two words, but they pierce deep into the soul, bring pain in the heart and rot, sometimes reminding us of itself.

Man cannot live without the assurance that he is loved, that he is needed, he languishes, exhausted , withdraws into himself, dies.

The worst crime we can commit against people is not to hate them, and treat them with indifference; that's the essence of inhumanity.

Please, never say «I do not care...»

Cain has seen the good that Abel did, and he said nothing. Differences that we refuse to honor, give recognition, turn into jealousy and end in fratricide. We cannot remain silent about the good, too! Observe people and recognize them, honor people!

When we are intolerant to others, when we do not tolerate other opinions except our own, we are depriving the world of the variety of colors, which it originally has. We are making our lives miserable and colorless, dull and empty. There remains only death, disappointment and scorched bare earth, mountains covered with the corpses of people we have "killed", albeit indirectly, but in the desire to ignore their differences. The clearest way to illustrate this is in the following parable by Anthony de Mello in the book «When God Laughs.»

In the middle of the XIX century American painter James McNeil Whistler took a short and unfortunate, from the aspect of academic education a period of training in West Point, the US Army Academy. It is said that when he was asked to paint the bridge, he painted,

A very original, stone bridge, connecting the grassy shore, and two young children, catching fish in it .

- Remove the child from the bridge! This is purely an engineering job! asked his instructor.

Whistler removed the children from the bridge, placed them to fish from the shore, and again showed the picture. An angry instructor yelled:

- I told you to remove the children. Totally! Take the children out of the picture!

But Whistler could not extinguish his creative fire. In the next version, the children were not in the picture, they were buried under two small tombstones on the riverbank. *[3]*

Here, collided together, a straight-line way of thinking, the pattern of action of an army officer, and a non-standard approach of a creatively gifted person. Once in the system of military education institution, where plain and monosyllabic answers are required, the artist was confronted with the fact that his view of the world was not understood and was rejected. The real world around us is not always as simple and straightforward as we would like. Ignoring the subtle nuances and details, we will trample the fragile relationships between people, allowing anyone next to us to become a victim of our callousness and heartlessness.

Ignoring or suppressing others' differences, not allowing differences of other people to open up and blossom, we are building tombstones on their souls and sending them away, out of lack of demand on their talents and gifts into the grave, having not found much need for their abilities. How many creative ideas and projects faded just because someone trampled on them with their boot of coldness, heartlessness, biases and prejudices. How many people have been considered a hopeless case, just because he who was close by, did not bother to see and honor their

differences. A lot of sad things happen when we refuse to understand the Law of difference.

In this chapter, dear reader, we have considered a most important matter, the consequences of a lack of understanding of the law of differences. We found out what can be worse than to go crazy, and who is Cain. In the next chapter, we will learn that success in life depends on the ability to see the difference. We will consider thanks to what modern business is built and how to create new products.

GOLDEN TRUTHS

The most terrible thing is when you recognize the difference in people but this makes you sick because the person has something better than you

When you are unable to celebrate a person, who has something better than you, then you are demonstrating the behavioral pattern of Cain, which is risking fratricide (killing your brother)

We behave like Cain, when seeing someone who differs from us, we ignore him in the best scenario, in the worst, we seek to kill them

Do not be silent when you see that somebody has been able to achieve something brilliant or excellent

All the good that are seen in people, should be recognized and verbalized

Whatever the difference, good or bad, always recognize it and never be silent

When we do not understand the law of difference, each of us individually and the society generally, are not ready to accept people who are not like others

SELF – ASSESSMENT

1. How often are you indifferent, that is, uncaring?
1) Constantly (0)
2) Rarely (1)
3) Never (2)

2. How much do patterns and stereotypes influence your thinking and behavior?
1) total influence (0)
2) 50/50 (1).
3) Minimal impact (2)

3. Does it please you, when your neighbor's in sorrow?
1) Yes (0)
2) 50/50 (1)
3) No (2)

4.Does it upset you when your neighbors are happy?
1) Yes (0)
2) 50/50 (1).
3) No (2)

5. Do you keep quiet about the merits of people, even when you notice them?
1) Yes (0)
2) 50/50 (1)
3) No (2)

EVALUATION OF TEST RESULTS

(0 points) We are sorry, but Cain does not only live in you, but reigns in your life. Most likely, you notice the difference of people, but what is terrible is that you get sick from knowing that he or she is better than you. You can read above, what this leads to. If you do not like this prospect, I recommend you take urgent measures to change the status quo. This book was designed to help you, so carefully study it.

(1 - 9 points) Not bad. Even though you found a Cain in you, you are trying to overcome this «invisible» enemy that wants to wipe out your humanity. Remember, «the winner is the wolf that we feed.» Therefore, «feed» not the beast in your soul, but the human of high standards and nobility, that would rather give their soul for the sake that the differences of other people might blossom in their entirety, rather than going to dance on the bones of those he was able to «eat» in clever conspiracy. Always, in all things remain HUMAN!

(10 points) Congratulations! Understanding the law of difference is your strength. That is why you manage to avoid all the dangers that threaten people who do not aspire to understand this law. This means that madness does not threaten you and you cannot become a killer of people, only because they are in one thing or another, better or just different from you. Share the perspectives of your vision or understanding of life with others, and it will bring you good fruit in your life!

GUIDELINES FOR THE IMPLEMENTATION OF PRACTICAL TASKS

1. CAUTION: These activities should not only be read and forgotten, they are VERY IMPORTANT. According to many years of working with people I know people often perform such tasks «for the sake of it" but it's your life, this is for you, take them seriously.

2. To maximize results, I suggest performing the tasks within the 24 hours, otherwise, you will forget, get distracted and you will distance yourself from the results you want.

3. To answer all the questions, find a quiet place and systematically work out the tasks.

4. Meditate on each chapter, on all the points that you underlined for yourself, reflect on the them and write out your steps of action.

5. Set yourself a time frame, constraints, to help you not to put off working on yourself.

6. Find someone you can be accountable to, who could help remind you to stay focused on working on yourself.

PRACTICAL TASKS

Rate your level of indifference on a scale of 0 to 10, where 0 is the minimum value and 10 is the maximum. To what conclusions does this lead you to? What are you going to do to change the status quo?

Consider how often you generalize things in your lives. How do you assess the magnitude of harm from these generalizations?

Give five examples from your life, when you behaved like Cain.

What consequences did that bring? What conclusions do you draw from this?

CHAPTER 8

SUCCESS IN LIFE DEPENDS ON THE ABILITY TO SEE DIFFERENCE

SUCCESS IN LIFE DEPENDS ON THE ABILITY TO SEE DIFFERENCE

The previous chapter was devoted to the consequences of a lack of understanding of the law of difference. In this chapter, we will look at principles of success that made Coco Chanel to be successful. You will know the secrets of the development of modern business projects. Most importantly, I want to pass over in this chapter that success in life depends on the ability to see difference.

The law of difference: **If you understand this law, you can achieve anything in this life.** Very much, if not everything, depends on the ability to recognize and see difference. This is what makes people great. Ability to recognize, distinguish, to discern, DIFFERENCE, this is one of the most powerful tools and skills that you can acquire in life. People who have the skills to recognize difference between things, between people, between places, between objects: they rule this world!

Those who become great are those wise men who know how to notice and see the difference, who live according to the law of difference. The ability to see difference is what life is built on. SUCCESS IN LIFE DEPENDS ON ONES ABILITY TO SEE DIFFERENCE. **Anyone who sees**

difference better than others, rises above all OTHERS in life. Do you like this statement, dear reader? You want to know, why this is so? It's very simple: if a person can recognize the difference, it means that they see something which other people do not see. People who see what others do not see reign on earth.

One of the most important achievements of your life, which you must constantly cultivate and perfect, is to become a specialist in how to see and discern difference. This applies to any profession. If you are the personnel manager, then engage solely in how to learn as much as possible to notice more perfectly the differences in people. Learn to study and acknowledge their strengths and contributions. If you are working directly with various groups of products, be engaged only to strengthen and further develop your ability to see difference between the products. If you are engaged in building systems, always look for the differences, the little details and nuances that can completely change the habitual way of life.

LAW OF DIFFERENCE – CATALYST FOR CREATION OF NEW PRODUCTS

- I will buy the iPhone 5 only
because it is the fifth!
Well, the slogan of Apple: "We are making millions on the
wish of the "hype» of the Youth" is still valid.
From an overheard conversation

Some argue that this is the translation of the phrase Steve Jobs said: «we earn millions on the» hype of the youths». The correct translation, according to the version of these people, is: «Others make and sell computers as computers, we make computers and give them style and people buy them for our style. We are making millions on the creation of style. «[19] In this case, the meaning is not the same as in the «show - off» version. Whatever it was, the greatness of Steve Jobs is his ability to see the difference. He saw no need to sell the device itself, many companies do that. He saw the need to offer the customer the style of life that they want. Actually, Steve Jobs became what he became, as a result of his ability to discern such nuances and minor details, differences that exist in current models of computers and phones. He carefully watched the development of the computer production industry and on the basis, that he saw differences, he took the decision to add or remove a particular component, making it possible to obtain a new product. This is the law of difference!

The «hype», we can say, that modern day industry is based on creating, the «rattles» or extras, which doesn't make much sense. If there is a sense at all, 99.9% of users do not use all the capabilities of these devices, because they simply do not need them. The manufacturer is interested in convincing consumers of the necessity and usefulness of these things. «One of these will be useful for you, make your life easier, more organized!", with this they convince the buyer, in reality knowing that many of these functions will remain untapped but this is the «hype»! It

is said, that Russia, located on the 57th place in terms of standard of life, ranks first in the number of iPhones per square meter, in commuter trains during peak hours. [20]

To force consumers to purchase on a regular basis, manufacturers are constantly improving their products, creating an artificial excitement around new models. They only engage themselves to find differences: what in this model differs from the previous one? What can you add to a new model? Thus, making minor changes, the producers manage to get consumers spend a crazy amount of money for an allegedly «new» model, which differs from the old only in some minor innovation. The market is always buzzing:

- *the latest model has been released!*

- *what's the difference from the old one?*

- *This was not in the previous model... is the answer*

The foundation of any successful modern business is the law of difference. The philosophy of modern business is constantly adding new changes to enhance improvement. If Apple had stopped with iPhone 5, saying: «Enough!" Then Samsung or another company would have forced Apple out of the market and in the following year Apple would be out of business. It is worth adding or make the slightest changes and announcing the release of a new model, and continue to make money, like from nothing!

How much is buying a new phone (smartphone) dictated by necessity? How often are we motivated to purchase a new model of a brand by the skillful actions of the brand marketing managers, the modern monsters of business? Are we really interested in it, or is it just the desire of producers to make money on the hypes of consumers? To the question: «how often do you change your phone (smartphone)?»The respondents answered as follows: [21]:

- I have an iPhone, and when a new model is released I immediately Run headlong and buy - 5.4%
- I have a smartphone manufactured by Samsung, I want the fifth model, I AM USING THIS ALREADY 2 years - 8.1%
- every six months - 2.7%
- ONE TIME per year - 16.2%
- every 2 years - 13.5%
- every 5 years - 37.9%
- I never change, all the buttons have FADED, and IT still works! – 16.2 %

The first mobile phone in Russia was sold in 1991. If you managed to be there at that time, you should remember that they were bulky tubes with monochrome displays that performed a single function: to call other subscribers. You must admit that by modern standards, this is not enough for a full-fledged phone. Today, when you buy a telephone, rarely are the buyers interested in a quality of communication. Most buyers scrutinize the functions of the devices that have gone far beyond a telephone. We're interested in playing audio and video files, the ability to access internet, do photo and video recordings, check email, view text messages, games, and much more. The last option games, for many has become the main indicator of general functionality of a mobile device.

The same thing goes for the automotive industry: all new models of cars Mercedes, Volkswagen, etc. appear only as a result of gradual addition of new details to make minor changes. In the production of clothing - the same thing! So, business in this world is driven by difference! Progress, the development of civilization is based on the search for and the ability to find differences, recognize the minor details, which result in a different product, and so ordinary or common things are perfected or new ones are created.

Any person who has achieved something worthwhile in this life, did so only by the law of difference, because they could see difference. Whatever you do, your priority is to do everything possible to observe what others do not see, the difference. To succeed in life, you must see what is missing in a product, what is in excess and what is lacking. Learn how to be sensitive to this kind of detail and seemingly insignificant things.

Valentin D from Kiev created a game and there is nothing like it on the Internet. There are still no equivalents to that which Valentine managed to do. What enabled him to achieve success in this area? He was looking for something that was not in other games. It turned out that his game, which, judging by the reviews of users, is still much liked until now. He achieved this success through an understanding of the law of difference. It played a key role in his life: in two years, he earned more than he could earn his entire life before his creation!

Please take very careful note of this principle: it will help you in any business you get involved in, no matter what you do. Compare two - three - four working models of your predecessors, find what is not there, add a little of your own special features and that's it! You will be ahead of all! You will get income where someone did not see the possibility. Jean Alphonse Karr (1808 - 1890), French writer and journalist, said: «to make a living, you must work. To get rich, you must come up with something else». To come up with something different, you must generate an idea. Even Napoleon Hill said: «Just one, only one sensible idea is what you need for real genuine success".

THE SUCCESS STORY OF COCO CHANEL

Fashion has two objectives: to comfort and love. The beauty arises when fashion achieves these goals.

- Coco Chanel (1883 - 1971),
French fashion designer

One of those who came up with something different, something that has not been seen, was the legendary Coco Chanel. She achieved outstanding success, thanks to the fact that she saw the difference between the way her contemporaries dressed and how they could dress. Her creed was to make clothes for women comfortable. Coco Chanel made women trousers, which brought them freedom, speed of movement, and invented the "little black dress", which every woman could afford, even a woman with more than modest incomes. «I am creating a Ford and not a Rolls - Royce», Chanel said, reaffirming her commitment to convenience and simplicity. [22]

With the elegant dresses from Chanel, women for the first time in many centuries, felt free. With needle and thread this amazing woman was able to reshape perceptions about feminine fashion and the rights of pregnant women. It is said that Coco Chanel triggered the era of the "self-made woman". Because of her achievement, no one can think of a woman as a helpless creature, who is not even able to dress herself, as a toy to fulfil all the lusts of men, but as a personality, able to earn money with the help of their own mind and talent. [23]

Who would have believed that a graduate of an orphanage school, whom nuns taught how to sew and embroider, would become a legend, and cause a revolution in the fashion world? The French fashion designer Coco Chanel (real name Gabrielle Bonheur, 1971), the fashion house Chanel, is said to have had a colossal influence on the fashion of the 20th century. Thanks to Chanel, women's fashion underwent modernization. Did Coco come up with something radically new? No, all her lifetime she played in an exclusively traditional male field. She just borrowed many elements of traditional male wardrobe. Chanel just saw how it could be used in women's clothing. She just carefully examined what was already known, saw the differences and introduced it into practice. Success was not long in coming. «I thought that I would need much more time to become popular, that it would be more difficult. Fortunately, it was fairly quick and easily achieved», said Coco Chanel. [24]

Initially, tweed and jersey fabrics were considered rigid, out of which you can sew only men's suits. Chanel imperatively broke this stereotype and created a female tweed suit, which became the epitome of luxury and elegance. [22]

She first started to mix jewelry and imitations. Coco Chanel did not like «stones for the sake of stones, like a sign of wealth of the husband or lover of women who wear them. I do not like jewelry for the jewelry, diamond earrings or pearls, which are removed from the safe to appear in them. They often belong to any run of the mill company»[23] She changed the idea about jewelry. Ornaments should be accessible, said the Frenchwoman. If they are real, it gives a bragging attitude, ostentatiousness. I'm doing a fake one and it's very beautiful. They are even more beautiful than the real ones. «[23] Due to applying the law of difference

Coco Chanel was able to see the value of jewelry. It existed before, but the she introduced it into use, giving it an unprecedented place in popularity. All because she could see the difference, which she gave to these ornaments.

Thanks to Coco Chanel also ended the era of singular perfume scents. The unusual fragrance Chanel No. 5 is a complex scent, consisting of more than 80 ingredients. In the minds of people, she to create a new idea of what should be the scent of a woman. Coco Chanel did not stop there: it changed the general idea of the purse. Before Chanel, women were forced to carry in the hands of handbags, which was inconvenient. It freed women from these problems, giving them a small quilted handbag on a long chain, which is convenient to wear on the shoulder. [23] Coco Chanel was not only involved in the creation of clothing, but also footwear. Mademoiselle did not change her style: she preferred comfortable shoes on a small heel. The first to offer a woman wearing two-color shoes: beige shoes with a toe in black patent leather, not only drew attention to its owner, but also visually reduced the length of the foot and lengthened the leg. [22]

You see, dear reader, the consequences of knowledge and application of the law of difference thanks to her. Coco Chanel created original new products which found a demand among her generation. Moreover, she managed the world of high fashion and entered the list of the top one hundred most successful people of the 20th century. [22] Coco radically changed every modern woman, even if she does not know about. All of that because Chanel saw differences in the familiar things.

THE ONE WHO SEES THE MOST DIFFERENCE RISES ABOVE

Coco Chanel conquered the world of fashion Olympus, due to the ability to differentiate, to see the difference. Where everything seemed ordinary, she saw the unusual, useful and necessary, she created for herself a name and great riches. She entered the history of fashion, leaving a memory of herself even after her death. Can you imagine a height, higher than the top of which Coco Chanel managed to conquer? **If you can see difference, you can rise very quickly to any level, starting with the lowest level and ending with the highest position that you can imagine.** Using the law of difference to your advantage, you will be able to overtake everyone who are, up till now still ahead of you.

If you are employed and demonstrate an understanding of the nuances and details in the various aspects of your company, then you will inevitably be promoted. If you can show with facts and figures in hand the details that can change the picture of the present happenings, that is do that which others do not pay attention, then rapid progress up the career ladder is guaranteed for you! Due to your ability to see the differences between even minor details, you will soon be able to take a leadership position.

NOTHING IS MORE IMPORTANT IN THIS LIFE THAN THE ABILITY TO SEE DIFFERENCES. This is the function of wisdom. With the ability to see the difference, billions of people make a lot of money. Using only one factor, an understanding of the law of difference, people become great, in their life comes prosperity and success. Think about what jewelers do. Think about what jewelers and bankers do. Their work, in fact, is to understand the differences between precious stones and money. The ACTIVITIES of jewelers and bankers are based on the knowledge of the law of difference, they live it. We all need to have someone who understands what is real gold and what is fake, what money is real and what is fake.

If you're a make-up artist or stylist, then through correct application of the law of differences, you can be original, exclusive in your sphere. If you do not limit yourself to how things are done everywhere, if you study the practices of make-up of styling for example, Indonesians or Hispanics, you can see the differences that exist in these cultures and their techniques. Based on the study, you can see something new, and it will help you create a product that is entirely different in quality from what is offered all around. Then you get the advantages that forges you ahead, leaving you far apart from the competition.

If you try with all of your strength to become a new word in history, nothing will be easier than to be the best in this field. Carefully study the experience of your predecessors, find out what was done to before you. Then find differences: what else is missing? what can be added? Get answers to these questions, you can create a product based on an understanding of the law of difference and create something that has never been done.

If you can understand the power of difference, you can reach incredible heights in any sphere. But it starts small: when you meet any person, look at what you can learn from them. What is their difference? What do they have that you do not? Recognize who you can learn from, just kneel, not physically, but in heart, in your attitude to this person. Whoever you come across, ask yourself the question: what is in this person, that I do not have? What can this person do, that I cannot do? What can I learn from this person? That should be your focus from morning to evening, it's how you enrich yourself. You create your uniqueness and originality, you become unique and different from others. IF YOU ARE DIFFERENT FROM OTHERS, YOU ATTRACT POSSIBILITIES TO YOURSELF.

«Real opportunities lie where no one sees,» said the businessman Jack Ma, whom I have mentioned in this book. That is, the ability to see differences, to discern, is directly linked to how often in your life new opportunities will come. Opportunities are conditions or situations that enable us to do or fulfill something. Often,enable us to do or fulfill something. Often, opportunities are like one of the ways at the intersection, you must choose on time from a variety of options. Before you show a quick response, you'll need at least to see this opportunity.

IF WE LEARN TO SEE DIFFERENCES, WE HAVE LEARNED TO SEE THE POSSIBILITIES. Because the difference between the rich and the poor is that the poor do not see the possibilities which a rich man sees. This is the major difference between them! The bible says that God gave eyes to the poor and the rich. What do eyes have to do with it? The eyes talk about the ability to see the difference, to distinguish. Therefore, one sees and multiplies their wealth, due to the ability to differentiate, the other sees nothing and remains poor. True, isn't it? Don't you find this interesting? I invite you, dear reader, to understand what real wealth actually is. This will be discussed in the next chapter.

With all the above we can draw the following conclusions.

1. **If you want to succeed in life,** then the law of difference is the first thing you need to learn and begin to apply in your life.

2. **Business development in todays' modern world is due** to the knowledge of the law of difference

3. **By discovering the power of difference one can** reach incredible heights in any sphere.

So, in this chapter we have found that success in life depends on the ability to see difference. In the next chapter we will talk with you, dear reader, how important it is to discover true wealth.

GOLDEN TRUTHS

People who have the skills to recognize difference, rule this world

The success of a person depends on his ability to see difference

Anyone who see the most differences, rises above all in life

People who see what others do not see, dominate on the earth

One of the most of important achievements in your life, which you must constantly cultivate and perfect in yourself, is to become a specialist in seeing difference and discerning them

The foundation of any successful modern business is the law of difference

If you can understand the power of difference, you can reach incredible heights in any sphere

If you are different, you attract opportunities; if you learn to see difference, you learn to see opportunities

SELF – ASSESSMENT

1. Your attitude to detail?

1) I'm distracted and inattentive (0)

2) I aspire to be a meticulous person, but often my attempts end in failure (1)

3) I am distinguished by a rigorous approach to everything (2)

2. How developed in you is the ability to see in the ordinary what is unusual or seeing a new application?

1) Almost not (0)

2) A lesser extent (1)

3) A greater extent (2)

3. Are you afraid to be yourself, to show characteristic features of yourself?

1) Yes (0)

2) 50/50 (1)

3) No (2)

EVALUATION OF TEST RESULTS

(0 points) Sorry. You are confident that the only reason why you have no success is lack of money. You are happy to give all your money for the latest phone model. You do not realize that somebody is just trying to make money out of your strife to be better than others. You lack the ability to discern difference in what you are doing, you are wasting your life and are poor. If you don't like this state of being, I recommend you read the next chapter of this book. In it, I am sure you will discover a secret that will you help you in a qualitative way to change your life!

(1 - 5 points) Not bad, you've understood that those who thrive in this life understand something about the law of difference. Only a small part remains, to emulate those that understand this law and to master the art of the ability to see and explore difference. Look at yourself and discover your difference. That is what will lead you to your desired success. This book was designed to help you. Study it carefully and learn from it!

(6 points) Congratulations! You have not relied solely on money when it comes to starting a new business. You can use the principles of the law of difference to your advantage. You are on the right track! As a result, this will bring you into new heights, both in professional and all other areas of your life. Being aware of your differences, you'll go far in life! Share your skills and abilities with the people around you.

GUIDELINES FOR THE IMPLEMENTATION OF PRACTICAL TASKS

1. CAUTION: These activities should not only be read and forgotten, they are VERY IMPORTANT. According to many years of working with people I know people often perform such tasks «for the sake of it" but it's your life, this is for you, take them seriously.

2. To maximize results, I suggest performing the tasks within the 24 hours, otherwise, you will forget, get distracted and you will distance yourself from the results you want.

3. To answer all the questions, find a quiet place and systematically work out the tasks.

4. Meditate on each chapter, on all the points that you underlined for yourself, reflect on the them and write out your steps of action.

5. Set yourself a time frame, constraints, to help you not to put off working on yourself.

6. Find someone you can be accountable to, who could help remind you to stay focused on working on yourself.

PRACTICAL TASKS

In what way can you apply the principles of the law of difference in your sphere of operation? How will your approach to work or activities that you do change after reading this book? In what ways can you achieve a breakthrough to a new level of achievement by applying the law of differences?

What lessons can you learn for yourself from the history of the success of Coco Chanel? Write 5 to 10 points that you can use in your life and activities.

CHAPTER 9

DISCOVER YOUR TRUE WEALTH!

DISCOVER YOUR TRUE WEALTH!

In the previous chapter, we found out that success in life depends on the ability to see difference. We elaborated on the following:

- What modern business is built on

- Law of difference - catalyst for creation of new products

- The success story of Coco Chanel

- The one who sees the most differences rises above the most

In this chapter, we will talk with you, dear reader, why it is important to discover your true wealth. First, we will look at what true wealth is. Then answer the following questions.

How do you convert your internal resources into tangible, visible material wealth?

Why do we need to find out what our differences are?

What will help us overcome our inferiority complex?

The origins of «Sisters of Mercy»

Thanks to Florence Nightingale (1820 - 1910) in our vocabulary entered an established phrase, «sisters of mercy» or Nurses. Going beyond conventional wisdom, a young lady from a prosperous British family went against the wishes of relatives and devoted her life to caring for the sick. This was a time when it was not accepted that a girl from a high society be engaged in any form of employment, not to mention becoming a nurse in one of the shelters of London. The care of the sick, presented a repulsive picture: the sick or wounded would gather in one room, where both contagious and non-contagious infections represented, where the people themselves were a group of foul-smelling bodies, the stench was overwhelming. A drunken nurse, who would sit idle at the bedside, of the sick was not uncommon.

From her youth, Florence was bothered by the questions, «Who am I? Why am I here? What is my purpose? « In 1837, when she was 17 years old, an amazing event took place, which helped her to make the right choice and subsequently lead her to fulfill her destiny. Taking a walk through the garden, she suddenly heard a voice, «you have to do something important and nobody apart from you has the strength to carry out this task". Lady Nightingale, indeed, managed to spark a real revolution in the medical sphere. What before her time seemed unthinkable, almost unworthy, elevated Florence to an extraordinary status. Thanks to this woman nursing became a noble profession and was also recognized as very important at the state level. Because of her self-sacrificing activity, mortality decreased and the attitude to the conditions of patients in medical institutions radically changed. She managed to change the attitude toward this profession, previously nursing was considered a dirty job, Florence Nightingale elevated it to the category of a mission.

The turning point in Florence Nightingales' life, was the Crimean war which broke out in 1953, England took part on the side of Turkey. The British dropped their troops on the Crimean Peninsula transporting them through Scutari, a specially created army base in Turkey, where a field hospital was also set-up for the wounded and they were evacuated from Crimea.

The catastrophic situation in this field hospital, i.e., lack of medication, outbreak of cholera and typhoid, stirred Florence and other Sisters of Mercy, 38 in all, to travel to Turkey, to Scutari. In six months of her work, the mortality rate, decreased to a record 2% from 40%.

After the end of the Crimean War, Florence Nightingale was celebrated in England as a national heroine. Queen Victoria also met with her for two hours and she approved the health reforms in the army, which were proposed by Florence. Her proposed measures were implemented at the state level, as a result of which the mortality rate among soldiers over the next three years went down by 50%. She released her published works on this subject and opened the first of its kind in history, a school, Sisters of Mercy. During her life, she refused a magnificent funeral in Westminster

Abbey. Founder of the international organization, Red Cross, the Swiss Henry Dunant said that the main inspiration of his organization was Florence Nightingale and her work during the Crimean War. [25]

Florence Nightingale gave up the wealth and luxury that she inherited by right of birth. She could have built a political party by marrying an aristocrat or became an intellectual or prominent poet and politician. However, Florence saw her true wealth not in the impressive condition of her father, William Nightingale, an aristocrat, Cambridge graduate and assured financial security. She was guaranteed a life of material and financial abundance. Driving around European capitals in luxury carriages with her mother, father and sister, Lady Nightingale noticed misery and poverty, children in rags. Visiting with charitable purposes (for girls in high society such visits were considered mandatory) one of the shelters on the outskirts of London, she was touched to her innermost being. Everyone who went saw everything, but only Florence really saw, discerned how she was the answer to their problems.

She could no longer remain the same Florence, her internal quality revealed in its entirety. Despite protests from the family and her father, who threatened to deny her inheritance, she rushed for the dictates of her soul. That which was resolved within her, was stronger and more important than money. None of the threats could stop her. When she followed her dream, money itself had to follow her. For her, money was collected throughout England and

WHAT IS TRUE WEALTH?

People for some reason think that they need money or other material resources to start something, to succeed in life. This is partly true. I tell you, money is quite still a limited resource: It basically comes to how much you have and it seems to disappear so quickly and at the end will finish. That is money, is a resource that can be exhausted, it is a limited resource.

Your internal resources which are part of your differences, unlike money, are inexhaustible. Money will sooner or later come to an end but my inner resources, my essence will never run out. If my strength is for example my emotion, then no matter how much I expend it, no matter how much I use this resource, no matter what I do, whatever I am doing, I'll be doing everything emotionally! Because it is my essence, this is me by nature, a part of me, it is impossible to separate it from me. It is inexhaustible: the more you spend this internal resource, the more it becomes. Or vice versa: I am not emotional and calm because I, I am a carrier of peace. From me emanates so much peace and quiet that even adults are lulled and sleep like babies. Your internal resources are much more powerful than limited material resources, including money.

Internal resources, such as a bright smile is an endless, inexhaustible resource. Why? Because God Himself has placed them in us. All that people have created, money and material things of course have limits, they will finish. That which God has given, has no limits, because it is something that lives within you. God is the Spirit, and the Spirit has no end, has no limits, no restrictions. Therefore, what the Creator put in us, His nature and essence this is the only thing that will always remain with you. You do not have to seek it, acquire or strive for it in any way. That which God has placed in us is the only thing that will never end, it is the only thing you will not need to worry about disappearing or going somewhere else.

Our problem is that even when we have something wonderful, outstanding, such as a smile, we are more concerned about what people think about us. We are afraid of public opinion: «what if they think I am showing off my abilities? What will they say about me? What if I am misunderstood, etc.?». We are afraid to agree with God in what He has bestowed upon us. As a result, we do not even use it. We do not believe in our differences. We think, «Well, what is so special, I'm so this, I'm so that, but I'm nobody". We nullify, bring to nothing, regard irrelevant, all that the Creator has done for us, investing in us His gifts and talents.

CREATOR SPENT HIS RESOURCES TO MAKE US GIFTED; SPECIAL TO GIVE US DIFFERENCE. We think that this is nothing! *"It is not money many would retort...*

Now if I had the money...", you are worried about money when you are already so excessively rich! We already have much more than money. We have neglected all these and reduced to zero, saying it is nothing, we do not even see what is already in us, we remain blind to the riches that are already hidden in us. **There is nothing more valuable than the ability to see differences discern.** God has ordained that the greatest wealth lies not in material things and money. What, then, is the greatest wealth? I'll tell you a secret: it is the ability to see difference. IF YOU SEE YOUR DIFFERENCES, YOU WILL FIND YOUR WEALTH. There is no greater wealth than the ability to discern the difference!

For example, I made a list of my strongest features. I know that the first thing that I have is passion. I am a passionate, emotional person. The next thing that I have is focus, the ability to focus my thoughts, all of those are inner qualities that make me wealthy as a person. I wrote down all these things making a list.

Our trouble is that we are not paying attention to our differences. You just need to find your difference and be sure that this is your unique difference! Begin to use it as your wealth. Because your difference IS YOUR WEALTH! Your difference is your money, your difference is your opportunity, your difference is your job, your difference is your own elevation! Do not forget that your difference is that which can make you famous. Your difference is what can lift you up, your difference is what you need, your difference is what you have been looking for all your life. How many people are searching for themselves but cannot find them self until the end of their days. YOUR DIFFERENCE - THAT'S ALL YOU NEED TO BE SOMEONE - IN LIFE! The law of difference - is the greatest gift you can give yourself!

On that day, when you see your difference and realize that these are your benefits, you will realize that this is your wealth, which will truly enrich you, bring you prosperity, success and elevation. Let me prove it to you. When you discover your difference, you will understand that any material resources, including money, is far inferior than what is hidden inside you. External wealth is at a lower level than the internal. Internal resources far outweigh material resources.

HOW TO CONVERT INTERNAL RESOURCES TO TANGIBLE MATERIAL WEALTH?

Any of your internal resources, even your smile can be turned into material resources. For this we need to approach people and just say hello, giving them a smile. Now everyone knows the image that we call "smileys" the styled graphic representation of a smiling human face. Traditionally, it looks like a yellow circle with two black dots, which represent eyes and a black arc, symbolizing the mouth. This logo is now popular because someone realized his internal wealth, a smile and today it is a billion-dollar business. Imagine that! a picture of the human smile, ☆, "smiley", generates billions of dollars in revenue!

For example, I know that my distinctive quality is a passionate approach to everything I do, I do all things with my full emotional involvement. What can I do with this? All that I need to do is to find a sphere and I will be successful there because of my inner richness. No matter what, I can do anything, business, because due to my inherent qualities, I will always be the best there, I'll always be successful. Why? Because I have the most important thing through which I will always reach success, it's me, my difference. When I found out for myself that my difference is passion, then to me, the rest is very simple. All that is left to do is to find a topic (sphere of action, task, vision) and start to « advance « it, using as an advantage my strong distinctive traits.

My main topic is my mission on earth for which I am living and for me it is that everybody knows there is God. I found this out when I was 19 years old and I think that is quite late. I lamented that I had wasted so much time, I bit my fingers, why didn't I know this before? When I realized that there is a living God, when I found out that everything written in the Bible is true, then I decided that I would give my life for it to convince the whole world about its misconceptions about God. No, I did not have the money. All I knew is that I had passion and emotion and I decided that I would use all my internal resources to open people's eyes to who God in reality is.

I came to Ukraine with 20 dollars in my pocket. Know what I started doing? I just started to meet people women, girls, boys, men, and their families. I started to do it on the streets, in parks and in public transport, everywhere possible, «listen, you may not believe it, but there is a God!». I told them just words, but as I spoke they started to cry and my words ignited their hearts. Although they did not understand a lot of what I told them because I did not speak fluent Russian at the time. It was not easy for people to understand me but they were struck by my sincerity, that they all asked one and only one question: What do we do? Just tell us what to do? Many of them followed me. In one year, I met with a lot of people, around 30,000 people!

That's what passion, not money provided me. The success in dealing with people, not material things made people to follow me. Passion is much stronger than money! Your inner wealth is much more than material resources.

We can continue my list of distinctive features. Next item on my list is focus, that is: if I start to do something, it is difficult to distract me, to force me to take my eyes off my goal. I persistently continue to beat at one point until I achieve my aim until I get my desired result. This quality is best described in the words of Jacob August Riis, pioneering social reformer: «when I look at a stonecutter, who hits the rock a hundred times with a hammer, without even a crack appearing but with the hundred and one hit with the hammer the rock breaks, I think the rock was broken not by the last blow but by their combination.» Is this not a magnificent picture of perseverance and focus? Namely this approach is indicative of me. I'll blow after blow until I achieve what I started for!

Therefore, no matter the topic I choose, and really, it does not matter which one, through my focus I will achieve success in any field! If your advantage is discipline, then no matter what you do, you can be the first there. These are the results inner wealth can bring you, even in the absence of material wealth which includes money. Do not neglect the true riches hidden inside you! Discover your difference and turn them into your wealth!

WHY DO WE NEED TO FIND OUR DIFFERENCE?

My dear reader, **one of the biggest victories that can be in your life, is the victory of discerning your difference.** If you can see your difference, what differentiates you personally, then there will be no heights which you cannot conquer, no breadth that you cannot embrace, no place that you cannot press in to! If you manage to see your difference, make a list of your differences, there is no top, you cannot conquer! It always comes back to one factor: If you can learn about your difference. Make a list of your differences, sit down, think and write down a list of these qualities so that they are always before your eyes.

IF YOU SEE YOUR DIFFERENCE, YOU WILL BE ABLE TO REACH UNPRECEDENTED HEIGHTS IN

LIFE. To see the difference in yourself is pivotal. In society, everything is directed that if you are not like everybody else then you must be shy, hide, feel timid, inferior, rejected, be filled with complexes and feel ashamed. What should we do? We should be a little adventurous and rebellious. The truth is, in the area where you are not like everybody else, **where it seems something is wrong with you in the eyes of others, where you are different from all others, that is exactly where your uniqueness is!** This is your distinguishing feature this is exactly the area through which God wants to elevate you.

To take advantage of the wealth that you have, make a list of your differences. Let's see Ina, a girl from a village not far from Odessa completed this task. Through a mixture Bulgarian and Moldavian blood, she looked amazing. The first thing she had to place on her list of differences were her eyes, eyebrows, eyelashes, dark skin, smile, teeth, dark curly hair, none of these features were like other people. Dear reader, if you have hair like Ina, then do not ever do what you probably do with your curly hair: do not straighten it! You know what to do in that case? If your hair is curly, it must be emphasized: «it is your distinctive feature!» Next on her list would be the culture she possessed because of belonging to this nationality, the temperament and character that had formed in her because in her veins, flowed the blood of those people of those nations, they helped form her emotions and internal values. YOU SHOULD ALWAYS EMPHASIZE YOUR DIFFERENCE!

Why do we need to emphasize difference? Because this is what I am! Everyone can be like everybody but I am different! Some are embarrassed that they stand out. That's no reason to feel uncomfortable. No! Your uniqueness is the object of your pride! This should line up with how you dress and behave. « I am here!" and this should be enough to make your uniqueness visible to all.

People who are different from the masses of people around them are a nice distraction in life that bring us a smile and warm, pleasant emotions. Why? Because they are different, they are not like everyone. Why don't you experience such feelings looking at other people? What you see always becomes common and boring, our eyes become accustomed and we no longer see the difference. If you're different, you will not become usual. This should be something to celebrate, to boast about, to be proud of and rejoice.

The question arises: how can your difference can help you? For example, how can the fact that you have unusual eyes, skin, friendliness, which not everybody has, an honest attitude to issues, how can this help you? First, your difference helps you to be confident, to overcome your complexes. Why is this important? Understand one thing: **if a person has a complex, about their appearance for example, then whatever wealth may be hidden inside it, these complexes will disturb and distract them and they will not be able to breakthrough in life!** I mean, because of complexes a person will stay on the sidelines, will try to keep a low profile, hiding and running away when the opportunity to come forward poses itself. COMPLEXES BASED ON APPEARANCE WILL KILL HUMAN POTENTIAL CONCEALED INSIDE. You never see the wealth that is hidden inside a person, when the top is covered, with a «thick» layer of complexes.

Therefore, it is important to emphasize everything: style of dressing, your look, make-up and hairdo, your unique temperament and character traits. Wherever I can find some advantage, where I can emphasize a difference, I must take advantage of it because all of this has far-reaching consequences: it will either help or block the release of your inner potential, your gifts and talents. It will either strengthen you, or nullify your slightest attempt to succeed. It will either help you get ahead and succeed in life or leave you among the outsiders and underdogs, where you will suffer, despite all your efforts, you will be wondering, "what Is wrong with me? why have I not succeeded?". Make a list of your differences, dear reader! Do not neglect this! This will help you in your life.

So, I'm sure that you are already convinced of the importance of knowing your difference by writing them on paper. Conduct an inventory of what you have, what God gave you, both in appearance and inner qualities. What should be done with the list of your differences you have made? Start to develop them and bring to perfection each of them. Study them, discover how you can use them to your advantage, how they can be useful to you. Then, strengthen, increase, multiply this difference, become the best in your sphere! Then next, offer your talents, your differences to the people who need them. For this, start to advertise your difference, your abilities. In the end, create marketing for your gift, sell it, sell your difference, turn it into a « Trademark» make money on your difference!

Michael V. has a difference: his height is not above a five-year-old boy! He was born like this, and it would seem, his whole life was doomed, to live and regret about his fate. From his childhood, his dream was to be a famous actor, in great demand. How can a person with a disability, by our standards, come into the circle of movie stars and show-business? Following norms and stereotypes (more on this in chapter 7), we would say no! Fortunately, this guy did not despair. He heard my messages and learned from me that our «uniqueness» can be our «trademark», through which we can realize our vocation and become famous and make money. What happened next?

After learning this valuable information for 1.5 months, Michael made his first-time appearance on television, and began his career as an actor. Now he is being invited by millionaires, folk artists and many successful television stations, clubs, directors and producers to work for them. He has already starred in commercials, music videos, movies, TV series and TV programs.

Is this not amazing? Because Michael recognized his difference and took the steps listed above, he went to a new level of life, a level he could not even dream of before. If he had continued to live in his problems, focusing on how poor and unfortunate, if he had remained in his comfort zone and was ruled by stereotypes, such a breakthrough in his life would have been impossible! After learning about the law of difference and beginning to live by it, Michael just blossomed before our eyes. He found a new destiny, new personality. Now his stunt physical feature is no more a disadvantage but his unique features that is rare to be seen. Today, thanks to his difference he is earning much more than many of quite «normal» people. Now after this example, tell me, is it worth finding out your uniqueness? I am confident that your answer would be Yes!

The next thing I want to convince you about, dear reader is that to find your difference is extremely important for you. «why is it necessary to find out what are our difference is? - You ask. Imagine what this kind of person would do when others suddenly do not understand them, judge or condemn their actions? I mean, they do not know where that person is going, they do not know about their purpose, objective and mission. A person who does not have a clear vision of their unique role on the earth, will find it hard to cope when others do not understand them, they will not be able to confront people and will be a victim of public opinion and judgement. Do not do that! do not go there, Stop!! All this because we are ignorant and in the dark about who we are and where we are going. The one, who knows what differentiates them from others, sees in this their advantage and uniqueness, a winning card, that can be used successfully when necessary, knows who they are and in what direction they are moving in life. They do not base their actions and decisions on the opinion of the surrounding people, even if they are the majority. For this kind of person, it doesn't matter what people think, because they know where they are going. The knowledge of self will pave the way, knowledge about self that is based on how God sees us. **Anyone who is aware of their uniqueness, has a light that is paving way for them throughout his life!**

Think for a moment about just how important differences are and the ability to recognize these difference in oneself. If you will work on investigating this, you find inner wealth that will never end, that will have no   limits and its supply will never end. You do not have to travel around the world in quest of it. Everything is hidden inside you! You only need to discover these riches.

WHAT WILL HELP OVERCOME INFERIORITY COMPLEX?

I want to tell you, dear reader, that when a person finds their differences, when they come to understand where they are different from other people, then often there is **an attempted attack to destroy these differences. What does this mean?** People around will begin to talk about you, about your faults, that something is wrong with you, they will begin to doubt you. This usually has a detrimental effect on a person, doubts start coming to them: "am I really wrong?" Doubt in your differences this is the attempted attack to destroy you, that comes from other people. This challenge comes to a person immediately after becoming aware of their differences. It is therefore important to gain confidence in who you are, be sure of your merits, which are your distinctive features. I also passed through similar tests.

When I walk down the street of a town in the former Soviet territory, because I have a dark complexion, I might encounter different responses because I differ from most pedestrians. Someone might just turn to look and follow me with their eyes, because they have never seen blacks before, for them I am an exotic brand. Another person might consider it their duty to insult me, calling me «monkey», «chocolate» or even «Nigger». Someone else might spit in my face, or even try to hurt me physically. Many of my compatriots rush to fight, because these negative attitudes ignite in them a feeling of resentment, and the desire to protect themselves and their honor and dignity. I want to tell you that similar attitudes of people in the streets of former soviet cities do not provoke me, I am not angry, not bitter and do not wave my fists when faced with such manifestations of racism. The fact that I already know my differences and inner wealth, helps me keep calm. That I am dark-skinned is just my external difference. Much more important is what is hidden inside me: my character, my inner qualities, love and compassion for people, care and attentiveness, responsiveness to others' pain.

I already know about my differences, I am not only not shy about them, but I do not also feel inferior about them, rather proud of them. If a person does not know anything about them self, what their differences are, what is their unique role why they are here on the earth, then by definition, they cannot be confident and have a healthy self-esteem. I want to say that self-confidence and healthy self-esteem arise from the knowledge about your mission, from the knowledge of those features which distinguish you. Anyone who is aware of their uniqueness, goes through life with their eyes wide open, not by guessing. If a person has no understanding of them self and their mission, then it means that they are blind, and on occasion this blindness will disappoint.

There are many like me, people who are dark-skinned and maybe, have internal dignity and values that could be of benefit to all the world, but they have not been able to establish in themselves, that to have differences, is not a disadvantage or a crime but instead a source of pride and advantage. So, they are not confident in themselves, do not love themselves, their personal difference does not excite them, they do not feel in connection with this joy and uplifting, it does not inspire and encourage them. Therefore, when society looks at them unusual, when other people look strangely at them, they are uncomfortable, they think that something is wrong with them. When someone looks at them crazy or says something bad about them, they start to take offense, get embarrassed, feel intimidated, lock themselves up and refuse to go out of the house. They lock themselves up in their own little world, that is they are bothered because they are different from others. The problem of these people can be solved very simply.

If they had «done their homework», compiled a list of their differences and began to work on themselves to impart confidence in their worth and significance due to their difference, then they would have seen great advantages in what they took earlier to be their disadvantages. These people would have been seeing their «pros» and then no matter what people would say, they would not have felt that something is wrong with them, that something is at fault in them. I have already done my «homework». I found my differences and understood their benefits. I saw my strength where others might consider it a weakness. I assured myself that my «uniqueness « is designed to give me glory, bring me elevation and security. Because the tests I faced did not pull the rug out from under my feet. I am self-sufficient, I do not need the approval of other people, to feel whole. If someone does not like me, it does not lead me into a state of despondency. The way other people look at me is their opinion. The main thing is that I know who I am, what my differences are and what are my advantages.

Many are concerned about the issue: how to not become proud? It's easy. *Pride is when I see only my difference. Pride is when I am not able to recognize or see the difference of others. When I notice, and appreciate my own differences, it's easy for me to recognize and evaluate the true differences of others.*

You need to be sure of you are, what differences you have. Respect your differences, your uniqueness. Why must we do this? Because your uniqueness is more important than your weaknesses, your «uniqueness» is more important than your weaknesses. Celebrate, appreciate, celebrate your differences, celebrate that you have them, because they adorn you! Do not build a cave from your weaknesses, don't engage in a pity-party about them, unfortunately some people live every day like this: «I am not so perfect, I am not good enough!» Do not Ridicule yourself and shed tears over your imperfections. This only leads to depression and nothing more. Such people are busy complaining that nothing in them is right, that they are not like everybody else, that they don't have this and that. It's not so important, what you don't have. **Much more important is what you already have.**

Keep focused on your difference. Make a list of your differences and develop them to perfection, work on them. Help yourself: Improve the advantages that you have. Do not focus on your weaknesses and shortcomings. What you can do with your weaknesses, is to deal with the problem, but do not dwell on them, do not cry, do not complain. Why is it important? Because that on which we focus becomes larger. **If you focus on weaknesses, they increase, if you focus on the advantages they increase.**

Seek to see how God looks at you. For this you need to write out the truths of the Bible that defines you, your new destiny, your new level. Start affirming them every morning before the mirror: "I'm smart, I am a genius, I am talented, I have the seed of greatness living in me!" We must begin to assert that which is according to God's view of each of us. We must, start to believe that God is not decorative art, a figurine. What He says, is exactly what He means.

Being aware of your differences, discerning them in yourself, knowing your strengths and weaknesses, absolutely even without money you can rise from the lowest level in life to the highest height, no worries, as from an office cleaner to the president of a multinational corporation in a very short time.

At the end of this chapter I recommend you summarize:

1. **Your most important resources in life are not always material things, but what is hidden inside of you.** Your prosperity and success in life depends on how you find them and discover them.

2. **If you want to really get rich in this life,** it is necessary to carefully examine yourself and discover your differences. That IS your wealth.

3. **Inferiority complex can stop your progress.** If you find your differences and establish their advantages for you, then you will have a free and healthy mind-set.

So, in this chapter, we learned how important it is to discover our true wealth. You now know, what is true wealth and received answers to the questions:

- How to convert internal resources to visible material wealth?
- Why we need to find out what our differences are?
- What will help us to overcome the inferiority complex?

In the next and final chapter, we'll talk about how important it is to find the courage to not be like others.

GOLDEN TRUTHS

Your internal resources, unlike money are inexhaustible

If you will see your difference, you will find your wealth

Your difference, is your own wealth, your difference, that is all that you need to be something in life

Any of your inner wealth can be turned into material resource

If you will see your difference, then you can reach impossible heights in life

In, that where you think something is wrong with you, through the eyes of others, where you are different from everyone, that is your «uniqueness»

Complexes, because of the outward look will kill a person and their potential hidden within, it will interfere, distract and disturb them from «breaking through « in life

Anyone who is aware of their uniqueness, has the light that is paving them a way through life

Self-confidence and healthy self-esteem is derived from the knowledge about your mission, knowledge about those features which distinguish you

If you focus on your weaknesses, they increase, if you focus on your advantages then they increase

SELF – ASSESSMENT

1. What is wealth to you?

    1) Money (0)

    2) Don't know (1)

    3) Me and my differences (2)

2. Do you emphasize the differences in your appearance?

    1) No (0)

    2) Sometimes (1)

    3) Without fail (2)

3. Do you suffer from an inferiority complex?

    1) Yes (0)

    2) Don't know (1)

    3) No (2)

EVALUATION OF TEST RESULTS

(0 points) We're sorry, your low self-esteem does not allow you to move forward. You do not consider as wealth your internal values, you think you are a poor and deprived person. If you do not change this destructive attitude toward yourself, you risk for the rest of your life, to live on the sidelines and not reach what you dream about. Affirm who you really are. Dare to recognize and appreciate your differences. You can read more about this in the next chapter.

(1 - 5 points) Not bad, you are on the way to gain confidence in yourself and beginning to appreciate your own differences. This will help you soon convert your inner resources into material. For this you need to do your «homework»: make a list of your distinguishing features and begin to focus on your strengths. Dare to live life as a unique personality, choosing the best path for your life. This you can read in the next chapter.

(6 points) Congratulations! Your differences make you happy, you really enjoy them, you «bathe» in them. You realize that in them lies your «uniqueness», which not only distinguishes you from other people, but can become your advantage, which can help you to climb to heights unattainable for many. We will meet at the top! Do not forget to take with you a team of your friends. Help them gain the same self-esteem and outlook on life, which you have.

GUIDELINES FOR THE IMPLEMENTATION OF PRACTICAL TASKS

1. CAUTION: These activities should not only be read and forgotten, they are VERY IMPORTANT. According to many years of working with people I know people often perform such tasks «for the sake of it" but it's your life, this is for you, take them seriously.

2. To maximize results, I suggest performing the tasks within the 24 hours, otherwise, you will forget, get distracted and you will distance yourself from the results you want.

3. To answer all the questions, find a quiet place and systematically work out the tasks.

4. Meditate on each chapter, on all the points that you underlined for yourself, reflect on the them and write out your steps of action.

5. Set yourself a time frame, constraints, to help you not to put off working on yourself.

6. Find someone you can be accountable to, who could help remind you to stay focused on working on yourself.

PRACTICAL TASKS

What did you learn from the history of Florence Nightingale? What are your conclusions from the story of this woman?

Prove that the internal resources are endless, inexhaustible, unlike material resources. What is the reason for this?

How did you understand how the internal resources can be turned into material? Please describe how the principle you discovered can be applied in your life?

Are you proud of your difference (in appearance, character, etc.)? If not, why? Why should we respect our differences, our uniqueness?

Why do we need to emphasize our differences? What hinders you from doing this? How can your differences help you?

What is the advantage of people who are different from others?

What is the danger of complexes to the releasing of inner wealth that is inside every human being? How can we overcome these complexes? What can help you?

Make a list of your differences. You should have at least 30 points. This includes your character, your internal content (for example, passion, temperament, figure, etc.). Conduct an inventory of your differences, bring to perfection each of them. Study them, discover how you can use them to your advantage, how they can be useful to you. Then, strengthen, increase and multiply these differences. Next: advertise your difference, sell your difference, turn it into a «Trademark» - make money on your difference!

Put into words the image that you want to look like. Write down what you want to become. Write down those affirmations with which you will daily «build» yourself from within.

CHAPTER 10

DARE TO BE UNLIKE OTHERS!

DARE TO BE UNLIKE OTHERS!

Well, dear reader, we have reached the last chapter of book called the "Law of Difference». We are approaching the end. I recall that in the previous chapter of this book, we found out how important it is to discover our true wealth. We have learned with you, what true wealth is and explored:

- *How to convert internal resources into material*

- *Why we need to find out what our differences are*

- *What will help to overcome the inferiority complex*

In This chapter, we will talk about what the desire to be "like all" leads to. We will discover elaborately, what awaits those who dare to be different. At the end, we will sing the «ode» to the glory of the weird, rebellious and the troublemakers. We will do this to assure ourselves of the importance of recognizing our differences and to cherish them.

When all the people are not different from each other, sees the world the same, they behave like a gray mass. What is a gray mass? The gray mass means that everybody act the same, thinks the same way, differences are not welcomed and perceived with hostility. Think about this, who remembers the names of people who were representatives of the gray masses? Nobody remembers them, they are just statistics. No names, no significant achievements, 70 - 80 years of an insignificant life, after which no trace remains. When we speak of the gray mass, none can be distinguished from the other, because there are no outstanding personalities.

For many, life boils down to, eat, get dressed-up, get a good job, go on vacation, clean the house, pay bills, find a life partner. Although, all these things are necessary and are a part of our earthly life, without an understanding of your unique mission and its fulfillment of this important task, life becomes plain vanity, that only creates the illusion that a person is extremely busy doing something important, this is the illusion of busyness but in the actual sense the person is engaged in survival.

A life that is lived out in this «rat race» reduces man to the level of a small screw in a system, which mechanically performs its function. In this role is nothing unique that sets apart a person from the crowd or makes them special. Therefore, people living according to the requirements of this world, are hard to remember. Usually, these people are just a "screw" in the system, a thumb tack, generally no one remembers them. Who remembers the names of the builders of communism, who in their entire life lived from paycheck to paycheck, from 9 to 5 at work, raised up children, and later grandchildren? They built a house, planted a tree and raised up a son. Living a life out of their mission turned them into «gray masses »: They were just a generation of factory-workers, replaced by another generation, so that no one remembers their names and surnames. What difference does the name of an ordinary third-grade educated miller, who spent his whole life standing at a factory conveyer belt make? These people account for about 95% of the population of the earth and they are ruled by those who do not bow to the dictates of the system, those who refuse to live by the principles they propose.

The System eliminates the personality, the individuality of humans. The System does not need a persons' gifts, talents and special abilities, their differences. The System of this world needs you when you are young and healthy, while it is still possible to drain you of all vital life juices. Once a person is old, sick and weak, having lost the power to support the system, they will be thrown out of the system into the so-called pension for another take to their place, one who is young and full of strength and energy. The System of the world, is interested that people, "cogs" of the system, bring forth as many children as possible so that they can take their place when they retire!

The System of the world says, "come on bear children and as many as possible", and for this reason, look suspiciously at those who are not in a hurry to bow to its norms, those who are different and stand out on the gray background. Who will rise up to man the machines in the factories? Who will take on the jobs in factories? This question is very much a cause of concern to those in power and therefore they offer all sorts of handouts for the birth of children to increase the population, who are mindlessly happy about this false "manna from Heaven". I mean the government handouts as incentives for people to produce more children, just to keep the system running.

How does the gray mass conduct themselves? How do people often respond to differences in our culture? «Why be different? NO, the main thing is not to stand out! Important! Do not be exceptional... « for example, when we come into a store, and if everybody is quiet, we follow suit, even when we feel like talking, we keep quiet, no matter what happens around us, we do not interfere. We enter into the underground public transport sitting quietly buried in a newspaper, though we sit side by side, the main thing is not to stand out. Wherever we are, we behave like everyone else: we come, we see and immediately get adjusted to the same program. The result is already clear: «merged with the environment.» We adjust, so as not to stand out, not to excel. The main thing for us is to adjust to the overall trend. We adjust very quickly. In my opinion, we do it faster than the speed of light: in a moment, we have already become what, and how is «acceptable»! Is it not like this?

But to adapt, to be like all, lacking the will to stand out, this is the biggest killer of personality, calling, aspirations, dreams and uniqueness that God gave you. To not be a gray mass, you need to live by the law of difference. When you see the difference, when you dare to be not be like everyone else, you no longer belong to the gray mass. If you can discern your differences, nothing can stop you! Because if a person knows, where they are going, nothing can stop them. THE WORLD WILL GIVE WAY TO THE ONE WHO KNOWS WHERE HE'S GOING!

People who dare to reject framework this world system proposes, who dares to see the world differently, those who can interpret the world differently as the majority, those who are not afraid of their differences and appreciate them, those are the ones who rise above the average level, where the majority of people are representatives of the gray mass. **Anyone who ventures to abandon the usual thinking, the familiar mindset, accepted norms, becomes in this way a person who dares to be different.** The fact that a person dare to differ, sets them apart from the crowd, from the general population, from the gray mass, this makes a person extraordinary, outstanding. Dear reader, do you want to be unlike everyone else, unusual, extraordinary personality, who clearly stands out? I Believe: Yes. But DON'T rush, listen, what awaits you!

THE FATE OF THOSE WHO DARE TO BE DIFFERENT

First, they do not notice you, then they laugh at you, then fight you.
Then you win.

- Mahatma Gandhi (1869 1948),
a leader for India's independence from Britain,
founder of non-violence philosophy

The first reaction you may not like is this: first, the crowd, the gray mass would say, «Peacock has come, where did they come from? Who do they think they are? Proud! Upstart! - just look!" they will say anything, maybe, they will even throw rotten tomatoes at you. They will throw all kinds of trash at you, just because you're not like everybody else, because you dare to differ.

«With my manner of dress, I drew the ridicule of others, but that was the secret of my success. I did not look like everyone else», describes CoCo Chanel the secret of her success. At the same time, it is also evident the price she had to pay for success: universal ridicule. To be not like everybody else is not always comfortable. If you are the tallest or the shortest in your environment, red haired, wear glasses or fat- it's your difference. You stand out, you cannot be missed or confused with someone else. Therefore, such people often become the object of ridicule.

People often tell me, «Hush! Behave more quietly! Shut up at least a little - a little! Do not be so bold to declare things!». People advise me, suggest to me, to be meek and be low profiled. People ask me If I am not afraid to so boldly voice my opinion. I want to tell you: «I care less about fears, because I have God in heaven. If God is for me, then who can be against me? I have no opposition, because if God is on my side, it doesn't matter who is not on my side, doesn't matter who is against me. « Listen, if God is on your side then it is better that he alone be on your side, even if all people are against you. Because, if God is on your side then you are already the majority! "one person with God on their side, constitutes the majority!" This is not my invention but that of Alexander Suvorov (1730 - 1800), the great Russian commander, military theorist, a national hero of Russia. What should I be afraid of? Jesus Christ Himself said, "why be afraid of those who can kill only your body? The lives of those who can kill your body, is not in their hands, it is in Him to whom I belong. They do not decide anything in the long run, He decides, so then what should I then fear? I need to be afraid of only one thing - HIM."

If a person is afraid to make a bold statement to express his opinion, it is only because he does not know himself. The one who has the courage to do it, who knows who they are in God's eyes, for what reason they were born, where they are going, where God is taking them, has the courage and bravery. Because it is based on the knowledge and revelation of them self, a person can be brave and behave freely as they believe, even if this contradicts the opinion of the majority. A person who does not know their destination, who they are and where they are from, will be afraid of unconventional, will be frightened to conduct them self in a way that is not conformed to the accepted norms. Because their self-esteem does not correlate with that of a confident person, confident of their purpose and mission, knowing they are not here accidentally.

Confidence and courage begins with what you know firmly: «There is no one like me!» But when I affirm myself like this, some react, saying, «This Sunday is not humble, thinks too much of himself, came here from Africa and began to swing right!» this is the way some people treat me. Until now, many do not accept me. Why? Because I'm doing something that is unusual for their mindset. In the real sense however, so should everyone behave them self, who wants to become somebody in this life, for those who the words, greatness, calling, mission are not empty phrases.

If you are ahead, you will be the first to come under attack. All eyes are fixed on you who is in front. Everyone watches you. Why? Because if you find yourself in front, all the others follow you. Your back is looming in front of them as a target. Many do not even see anything but your back. Therefore, if you are different, your back is completely open for any comments, jokes, ridicule, and more often, the vicious and aggressive are the ones directly behind you. All can watch what you're doing.

But I want to remind you, dear readers, the words of Gaston De Lewis (1764 - 1830), French politician and aphorist: «Envy aggressively attacks the highest of virtues and spares only mediocrity.» MEDIOCRITY DOES NOT STIR UP CONTROVERSIAL FEELINGS. Strong emotions can be stirred up only by that which is out of the ordinary. It's no secret: that it is exactly what annoyed and provoked fierce debate among contemporaries, that is valued and revered by following generations as an outstanding achievement.

Niccolo Paganini (1782 - 1840), Italian composer, violinist and guitarist - virtuoso, owns two great quotes:

«The talented man is not loved and the genius is hated»

«The skilled are envied, the talented are hindered, the brilliant – are fought against»

Ralph Waldo Emerson (1803 - 1882), American poet, philosopher, pastor and social activist; One of the most popular thinkers of the United States, added, "you can recognize a true genius in that, at his appearance or the mention of his name, all the fools conspire against him". What is your strong trait, your gift, your talent, that can make you into a household name forever? This is exactly what irritates people around you, if they do not take the law of difference into consideration. But do not worry about this. Fyodor Dostoyevsky (1821 - 1881), one of the most significant and well-known world thinkers, said: "If you aim at a goal, and you start stopping on the road to throw stones at every barking dog, then you will never reach your goal". Even if you hear insulting words directed at you, it's not worth it to be upset or despondent. Keep your heart free from any hatred and anger and learn to forgive, that's what will make you stronger. «Do you want to become stronger - learn to forgive. You want to become even much stronger - learn not to be offended", said Tadao Yamaguchi, lecturer, writer, entrepreneur. To differentiate yourself and not be like others, you need to be strong.

Mother Teresa wrote the following in a kind of testament.

People are unreasonable, illogical and self -centered, forgive them anyway.

If you show kindness, and people accuse you of secrecy, of personal motives, show kindness anyway.

If you succeed, you may see a lot of imaginary friends and true enemies, succeed anyway.

If you are honest and frank, people may cheat you, be honest and frank anyway.

What you have built over the years, can be destroyed overnight, continue to build anyway.

If you have found a serenity and happiness, then you may be envied, be happy anyway.

The good you have done today, people will forget tomorrow, do good anyway.

Give the world the best of what you have and it will never be enough, continue to give them your best anyway.

In the final analysis, you will discover that this was between God and you, and never between you and them anyway.

Remember that that which happens between you and people, in the actual sense happens at a different level than we can see and the level of these relationships has more to do with you and your direct relationship with God.

From this point of view, there is a completely different meaning between what you are doing and what is being done against you.

No matter how long the ridicule, shame and spitting may last, it cannot last forever. In the Words of Mahatma Gandhi, who formulated the philosophy of non-violence and influenced the movement of supporters of peaceful change: "first they ignore you, then they laugh at you, then they fight you and then you win." The Night cannot last forever. No matter how dark it may be, sooner or later there comes the dawn. First, they ignore you, then laugh and scoff, and the fight you. But at the end of it…you win! This is the victory of a personality with unique features over the oppression of the gray crowd, trying to force you to march «like everybody else».

«PRAISE TO THE CRAZY ONES, MISFITS, REBELS, TROUBLEMAKERS. ...»

"Here's to the crazy ones, the weirdos, the misfits, the rebels, the troublemakers, the round pegs in the square holes... the ones who see things differently — they're not fond of rules... You can quote them, disagree with them, glorify or vilify them, but the only thing you can't do is ignore them because they change things... they push the human race forward, and while some may see them as the crazy ones, we see genius, because the ones who are crazy enough to think that they can change the world, are the ones who do."

Steve Jobs (1955 - 2011),
American entrepreneur, co - founder of Apple

The ability to be different, stand out, is one of the most powerful things that can happen to you in this life! There is nothing more precious than to not be like others. If you can be different from all, if you can withstand the negative consequences of your uniqueness, if you agree to be different from everyone, it means that you:

- HAVE AGREED TO DO WHAT HAS NEVER BEEN DONE

- AGREED TO BECOME THAT WHICH NO ONE HAS YET BECOME

Remember: there is no success without a desire to be different! Success is a synonym for «contrast». Becoming great means to be different! Becoming successful means to be different! Becoming the first - means to be different! Becoming the top, most top means to be different.

Nothing keeps people from success like fear: *«what if they do not understand? what if I get it wrong? and if this? If that?».* There is nothing more paralyzing than fear. If you have agreed to differ, it means you have overcome the fear by the name of «and if?» If you have defeated the fear of «and if?» this means that you are ready to become crazy and weird, you're ready for any move, ready to take any risk. That is, you will be ready to do anything to achieve your goal. This is what the ability to differ delivers to you.

«Keep away from people who try to belittle your ambitions. Small people always do that, but the really great make you feel you can become great», Mark Twain (1835 - 1910), American writer, journalist and public figure. If you want to retain your difference, your uniqueness, avoid being trampled by the gray masses, who demand you be like all others, then run away from those who steal your confidence, who sow in you, thoughts of insignificance, uselessness and futility. This is usually an indicator of how shallow a person is. Small minded people want to bring down all to their level.

As Les Brown, born 1945, American motivational speaker, author, radio DJ, former politician, said, «the opinion of others about you does not have to become your reality." This applies in the first place to the negative opinion about you, which are sown into your mind only to: oppress you, destroy your dreams and desires to reach the goal set by you, intimidate you or diminish the value of your differences, your unique gifts and talents. Great men allow others to grow by their side. Thanks to their own greatness they inspire everyone around them to have confidence that they too, can do it. Strive to get into this kind of environment, because only in such an environment, will your differences be genuinely appreciated and allowed to flourish like bright colorful flowers.

If you decide to be different and are willing to endure ridicule, misunderstanding, bullying, then it means you are ready to get to the end, you are ready to be the first and not the last. What does it mean to be the first? Being the first and not wanting anything different from the gray mass, to not stand out against its background – are two completely different things. Those who dare to be different, Steve Jobs called:

Crazy

rebels

troublemakers

Misfits

He described them as those who:

- *are always odd and out of place*
- *see the world differently*
- *do not follow the rules*
- *have no respect for the status-quo*

This is the quality that differentiate those who desire and are ready to be first, who dare to do that which no one has done, who dares to become what no one else has become. People like this, no doubt, deserve praise. Jobs was right in saying that these people should be quoted, they cause the most controversy and disagreement. They are so controversial that today, songs of praise are written about them and are highly esteemed to the heavens, and the next day are cursed and crucified. The only thing that cannot be denied is the fact that to ignore such people is impossible. They are always like the uncomfortable stone caught in the shoes, attracting attention to itself.

The most important thing is that these people, according to the original description by the words of Steve Jobs, «carry changes» and «push the human race forwards." At a time when some see them as weirdos, wise people see them as geniuses. For whom the law of difference is not an empty sound, discern such people and do not pass them b. Stop next to them to learn. Do not neglect these people, even if relating with them proves uncomfortable. Such people are definitely not part of the gray mass, they are personalities in the BIG SENSE OF THE WORD, they are actively changing the world.

Finally, I want to suggest to you, dear reader, the following theory:

Theory of the bucket with crabs

The Term «crab mentality» is used to describe the selfish, shallow-thinking that are programmed like this : «if I cannot then you cannot .» This term is widely used particularly in the Philippines. The locals refer to people who pull other people down, not letting them get ahead and reach their goal. This concept is taken from the beginning of an interesting phenomenon, which later became known as the «Theory of the buckets of crabs.» Here is the meaning. Crabs are such petty creatures, that when one of them is trying to get out of a bucket, others pull him back. Sometimes crabs show their anger in that they pull down at the last moment, when the crab almost reached the edge of the bucket.

When a person is trying to quit smoking, and friends say, «You won't make it" and gives them a cigarette, this is 'the bucket with crabs'. When you are getting a second degree, and colleagues loudly wonder why you need it, they say you are too tired because of your work, this is 'the buckets of crabs'. When your own parents tell you that you are (loser, average, nothing good will come out of you, etc.), yes - yes, this is again the 'bucket of crabs'. It is human nature, and you can do nothing about it, except one thing, **be Stronger THAN THE «buckets» and push forward, even when you ARE pulled back by a hundred people.**

If you accept the fact that you are different from the rest, then you have « given « yourself to conquer, to thrive, you have «humbled yourself « to reach and climb up as no one has ever done in this life! If you dare, if you agree to differ from the others - nothing will stop you!

GOLDEN TRUTHS

When people are no different from each other, see the world the same way, they behave like a gray mass

The System nullifies the individuality of a person

To adapt, to be like everyone else, have no desire to be different - this is the biggest killer of individuality, personality, callings, aspirations, dreams, and uniqueness

The whole world will give way to a person who knows where they are going!

Anyone who ventures to abandon the usual thinking, the familiar mindset, accepted norms, becomes a person who dares to be different

If a person is afraid to make bold statements, speak out their opinion, it is only because they do not know them self

Mediocrity does not cause controversial emotions

Strong emotions can be stirred only by that which is out of the ordinary

Success is a synonym for «contrast». Becoming great - means to be different! Becoming successful - means to be different! Becoming the first - means to be different!

If you can be different from all, it means that you:

- Have agreed to do what has never been done
- Can be someone that no one has become

SELF - ASSESSMENT

1. Are you willing to endure ridicule, humiliation, and misunderstanding to preserve your distinctions?

> 1) No (0)
>
> 2) Not Sure (1)
>
> 3) Yes (2)

2. Are you ready to reject accepted norms, mindsets and behavioral patterns?

> 1) not prepared (0)
>
> 2) 50/50 (1).
>
> 3) 100% ready (2)

3.How often are you intimidated by the fear «and if? and if they do not understand? and what if I get it wrong? and if …?"

> 1) Constantly (0)
>
> 2) From time to time (1)
>
> 3) Almost never (2)

4. Do you easily «adjust» to general opinion, general trend, following accepted norms?

> 1) Easily (0)
>
> 2) Sometimes (1)
>
> 3) Hardly ever (2)

5. How much does your heart connect to this slogan: «the main thing is not to stand out?

    1) 100% (0)

    2) 50/50 (1)

    3) Not at all (2)

EVALUATION OF TEST RESULTS

(0 - 3 points) We're sorry, you find it hard to believe that you need to stand out from others. You can easily succumb to another persons' opinion of you and it often turns out to be negative, which has a destructive effect on all areas of your life. That's why you're so far away from success, to being great and becoming the first in something. Even if you do not mind being someone no one has ever become, you are not ready to pay the price for it, you are not ready to be the object of everyone's attention and get hit by the opinions of others and gossip. If you do not want to live a gray life, if you want to change the color of your life from gray to something more, you should learn to draw self-confidence and assurance, you should build yourself and your inner values, your wealth. Read this book again and work through all the tasks to turn your dreams into reality! [15]

---

[15] The destructive - aimed at the destruction, disruption of the functioning of which - either.

(4 - 9 points) Not bad, you understand that self-confidence and boldness is needed to dare to be different from others, starting with the fact that you can express yourself with all boldness and categorically say: «There is no one like me!» Personally, you still lack such qualities, but you are on the right path, you realize what you need. You don't want to be part of the detestable gray mass, you do not want to share the lives of most people on this planet. Most likely, you want to stand out, but do not always have the courage to defend your right to be original. This book was designed to help you fulfill your dreams. Study it from beginning to end, and it will add confidence to you, to learn to really appreciate your differences and that of the people around you.

(10 points) Congratulations! Like Coco Chanel, you can readily say: «I do not care what you think of me. I am not thinking about you at all». This indicates that you are a confident person, you are not afraid to stand out from the crowd, especially stand out from the gray mass and you are not afraid to confront them all. You are difficult to distract, you stubbornly go towards your goal, because you know who you are. It's true: the world will give way to a person who knows who they are and where they are going. If that's you, then I can congratulate you, because, we will soon hear about you! In the meantime, let your ability help others gain self-confidence; to help them dare to be someone who is unlike others and who appreciate their own differences and celebrate others.

GUIDELINES FOR THE IMPLEMENTATION OF PRACTICAL TASKS

1. CAUTION: These activities should not only be read and forgotten, they are VERY IMPORTANT. According to many years of working with people I know people often perform such tasks «for the sake of it" but it's your life, this is for you, take them seriously.

2. To maximize results, I suggest performing the tasks within the 24 hours, otherwise, you will forget, get distracted and you will distance yourself from the results you want.

3. To answer all the questions, find a quiet place and systematically work out the tasks.

4. Meditate on each chapter, on all the points that you underlined for yourself, reflect on the them and write out your steps of action.

5. Set yourself a time frame, constraints, to help you not to put off working on yourself.

6. Find someone you can be accountable to, who could help remind you to stay focused on working on yourself.

PRACTICAL TASKS

Rate YOUR belonging to the «crazy, rebels, troublemakers and misfits» (in the words C. Jobs) on a 10 - point scale, where 0 is the minimum value and 10 is the maximum. How much does this saying of Steve Jobs about these people, describe who YOU are? What do you plan to do with the results of this self-examination?

How often in your life's journey do you meet people with the «crab mentality» that pulls you back from your dreams, disappointing and depriving you of self-confidence and inner strength? Develop a strategy to deal with them. How will you stop others from stealing your dreams and taking away your unique purpose and calling?

CONCLUSION

You may know, dear reader, the lines of the famous song by Leonid Agutin:

Vanity, shadow of light, the day draws near to the night,
Multicolored birds chirping outside the window.
And the moon in pure white above me and above you
Flip on fire flashed highlights.
And there is not nothing, it's not a dream or delirium,
Do not be afraid, he's good, though, and unlike us.
Unlike you, unlike me,
Just like a passer - a black man.
Unlike you, unlike me,
Just like a passer - a black man.
You're afraid of everything, and there is nothing terrible:
Just a guy like the guy, but a bit darkish.
And sometimes farther south, one other dark,
Where the trees grow, and bananas, and agate.
And there is not nothing, it's not a dream or delirium,
Do not be afraid, he's good, though, and unlike us.
Unlike you, unlike me,
Just like a passer - a black man.

✳ ✳ ✳

The song says that often in our lives we will meet people different from us, very different from us, people in terms of race, character, temperament or other traits. The problem of society is that we are not prepared to meet with the difference of others and successfully cooperate with those who are not like us. Most of the time we do not even want to notice the uniqueness and originality of the people near us, not to mention appreciating their true worth. When we don't know how to do this, it has a devastating impact on our lives: we become intolerant, declaring "war on the witches", persecute and even destroy those who are different or not similar to us.

Unfortunately, we were not taught to notice the uniqueness of each other, basically we were taught to live and to «wallow» in our own soup. We were taught to look only at ourselves, to worship ourselves. Many of us have an idol: self, we worship self, which is expressed in narcissism. Because we are too busy, we often fail to notice the uniqueness and differences of others. It's a disaster! It is not only a legacy of the soviet past it's the same, all around the world.

That's why this book was written: that each of us could develop a tolerance toward other people, so that we become more patient to the expression of the uniqueness and diversity of each person. The desired outcome of this book and the author is that we become a society, which understands and accepts others despite their differences, where people do not seek what distinguishes one from the other in a negative sense. Also, that we all become people that seek only to commemorate and celebrate the differences between people.

REFERENCES

1. « The «Choice» - https: / / ru.wikipedia.org / wiki /% D0% 92% D1% 8B% D0% B1% D0% BE% D1% 80

2. «the harm of McDonald's » - http: / / medicena.ru / / vred - makdonaldsa /

3. Mello e. «when God laughs»

4. D Kehoe. «the subconscious mind can do anything»

5. F. Zimbardo and M. Lyayppe. «social influence»

6. Sobolev F. «I and other» documentary, фильм, 1971, «Kievnauchfilm»

7. « Experiment Asha » to: / / ru.wikipedia.org / wiki /% D0% AD% D0% BA% D1% 81% D0% BF% D0% B5% D1% 80% D0% B8% D0% BC% D0% B5% D0% BD% D1% 82_% D0% 90% D1% 88% D0% B0

8. But Babitsky.. A Warriors.. The «miracle of Alibaba: how a former teacher created a business worth $231 billion » - http: / / / market / 562949992419026

9. A Makarov.. And Cherkasov. If the stars were put-off » - http: / / / booknik.ru / / history - of - protest / esli - zvezdy - gasyat /Phrasebook of Russian literary language

10. «scientists have found out why the Chinese for us all have one face» - Utro.ru - http: / / / www.mtio.com / articles / 2007 / 08 / 16 / 672105. shtml

11. «All with one face « - Novaya Gazeta - 26 November 2013 - http: / / / articles / /Russian Dictionary of Synonyms

12. «what we see and hear» - a parable as presented by Osho. Source: http: / / pritchi.ru / id_2355

13. Great personalities. Mother Teresa - http: / / nowimir.ru / DATA / 030,015. htm

14. «biography of Mother Teresa. Great Mission «- Purpose and implementation of human - http: / / prednaznachenie - cheloveka.com / biografiya - materi - terezyi.html

15. «the power of stereotypes. Washington ProFile, 2005 - http: / / psyfactor.org / lib / stereotype.htm

16. «two guys of different nationalities are asking for help with the same sign... The reaction of people is mind boggling ! » - Http: / / ofigenno.cc / pomoshch - lyudyam - raznoy - nacionalnosti

17. Answers @ mail.ru - http: / / otvet.mail.ru / question / 58893775

18. Mustache Peskov on Twitter - https: / / twitter.com / Sandy_mustache / status / 4539713221930598840

19. Answers @ mail.ru - http: / / otvet.mail.ru / question / 170655868

20. E Borisov. « in 7 creations of Coco Chanel that forever changed the fashion. «» Arguments and Facts «19 / 08 / 2013 - http: / / www.aif.ru / dontknows / about / 1236483

21. About Solovyov. «10 interesting facts about Coco Chanel » - http: / / www.woman.ru / fashion / medley3 / article / 90203 /

22. Biography of Coco Chanel. Internet - bank: http: / / / / designers /% D1% 88% D0% B0% D0% BD% D0%% D0% BB% D1% 8C -% D0% BA% D0% BE% D0% BA% D0% BE)

23. And Maximov. «Florence Nightingale: sister of mercy, sister of peace »

24.http://diletant.ru/articles/17706150/?sphrase_id=1029707

SUNDAY ADELAJA'S
BIOGRAPHY

Pastor Sunday Adelaja is the Founder and Senior Pastor of The Embassy of the Blessed Kingdom of God for All Nations Church in Kyiv, Ukraine.

Sunday Adelaja is a Nigerian-born Leader, Thinker, Philosopher, Transformation Strategist, Pastor, Author and Innovator who lives in Kiev, Ukraine.

At 19, he won a scholarship to study in the former Soviet Union. He completed his master's program in Belorussia State University with distinction in journalism.

At 33, he had built the largest evangelical church in Europe — The Embassy of the Blessed Kingdom of God for All Nations.

Sunday Adelaja is one of the few individuals in our world who has been privileged to speak in the United Nations, Israeli Parliament, Japanese Parliament and the United States Senate.

The movement he pioneered has been instrumental in reshaping lives of people in the Ukraine, Russia and about 50 other nations where he has his branches.

His congregation, which consists of ninety-nine percent white Europeans, is a cross-cultural model of the church for the 21st century.

His life mission is to advance the Kingdom of God on earth by raising a generation of history makers who will live for a cause larger, bigger and greater than themselves. Those who will live like Jesus and transform every sphere of the society in every nation as a model of the Kingdom of God on earth.

His economic empowerment program has succeeded in raising over 200 millionaires in the short period of three years.

Sunday Adelaja is the author of over 300 books, many of which are translated into several languages including Russian, English, French, Chinese, German, etc.

His work has been widely reported by world media outlets such as The Washington Post, The Wall Street Journal, New York Times, Forbes, Associated Press, Reuters, CNN, BBC, German, Dutch and French national television stations.

Pastor Sunday is happily married to his "Princess" Bose Dere-Adelaja. They are blessed with three children: Perez, Zoe and Pearl.

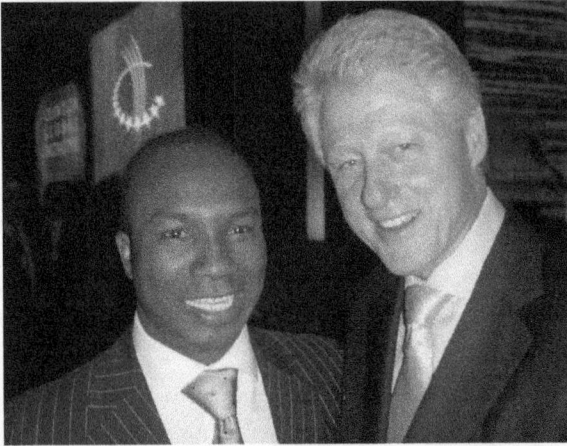

Bill Clinton —
42Nd President Of The
United States (1993–2001),
Former Arcansas State
Governor

Ariel "Arik" Sharon —
Israeli Politician, Israeli
Prime Minister (2001–2006)

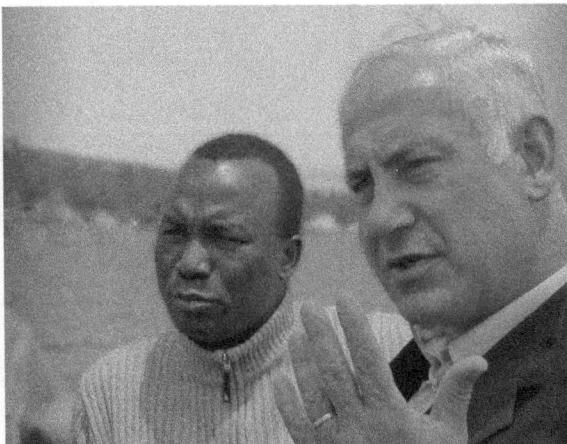

Benjamin Netanyahu —
Statesman Of Israel. Israeli
Prime Minister (1996–1999),
Acting Prime Minister
(From 2009)

Jean ChrEtien —
Canadian Politician,
20Th Prime Minister Of
Canada, Minister Of Justice
Of Canada, Head Of Liberan
Party Of Canada

Rudolph Giuliani —
American Political Actor,
Mayor Of New York Served
From 1994 To 2001. Actor
Of Republican Party

Colin Powell —
Is An American Statesman
And A Retired Four-Star
General In The Us Army,
65Th United States Secretary
Of State

Peter J. Daniels —
Is A Well-Known And
Respected Australian
Christian International
Business Statesman Of
Substance

Madeleine
Korbel Albright —
An American Politician And
Diplomat, 64Th United States
Secretary Of State

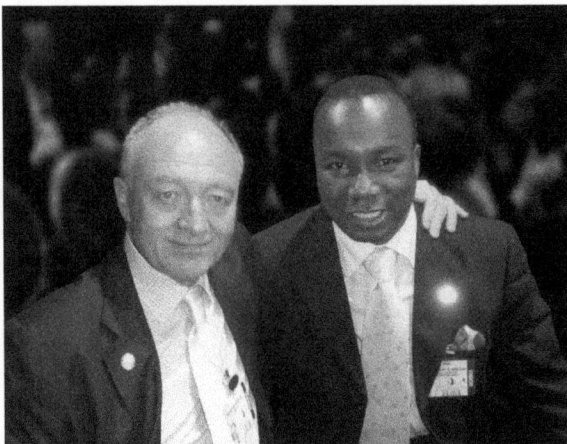

Kenneth Robert
Livingstone —
An English Politician,
1St Mayor Of London
(4 May 2000 – 4 May
2008), Labour Party
Representative

Sir Richard Charles Nicholas Branson — English Business Magnate, Investor And Philanthropist. He Founded The *Virgin Group*, Which Controls More Than 400 Companies

Mel Gibson — American Actor And Filmmaker

Chuck Norris — American Martial Artist, Actor, Film Producer And Screenwriter

Christopher Tucker —
American Actor
And Comedian

Bernice Albertine King —
American Minister Best
Known As The Youngest
Child Of Civil Rights Leaders
Martin Luther King Jr. And
Coretta Scott King Andrew

Andrew Young — American
Politician, Diplomat, And
Activist, 14[Th] United States
Ambassador To The United
Nations, 55[Th] Mayor Of
Atlanta

General Wesley Kanne Clark — 4-Star General And Nato Supreme Allied Commander

Dr. Sunday Adelaja's family: Perez, Pearl, Zoe and Pastor Bose Adelaja

FOLLOW
SUNDAY ADELAJA
ON SOCIAL MEDIA

Subscribe And Read Pastor Sunday's Blog:
www.sundayadelajablog.com

**Follow these links and listen to over 200
of Pastor Sunday's Messages free of charge:**
http://sundayadelajablog.com/content/

Follow Pastor Sunday on Twitter:
www.twitter.com/official_pastor

**Join Pastor Sunday's Facebook
page to stay in touch:**
www.facebook.com/
pastor.sunday.adelaja

**Visit our websites for more
information about Pastor
Sunday's ministry:**
http://www.godembassy.com
http://www.
pastorsunday.com
http://sundayadelaja.de

CONTACT

FOR DISTRIBUTION OR TO ORDER
BULK COPIES OF THIS BOOK,
PLEASE CONTACT US:

USA
CORNERSTONE PUBLISHING
info@thecornerstonepublishers.com
+1 (516) 547-4999
www.thecornerstonepublishers.com

AFRICA
SUNDAY ADELAJA MEDIA LTD.
E-mail: btawolana@hotmail.com
+2348187518530, +2348097721451, +2348034093699

LONDON, UK
PASTOR ABRAHAM GREAT
abrahamagreat@gmail.com
+447711399828, +441908538141

KIEV, UKRAINE
pa@godembassy.org
Mobile: +380674401958

BEST SELLING BOOKS BY DR. SUNDAY ADELAJA
AVAILABLE ON AMAZON.COM AND OKADABOOKS.COM

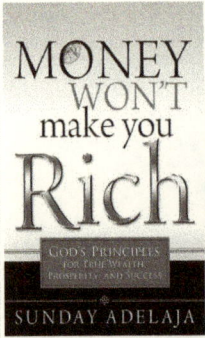

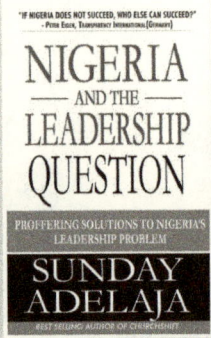

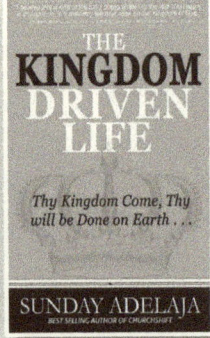

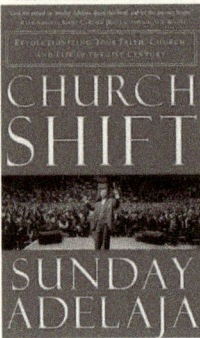

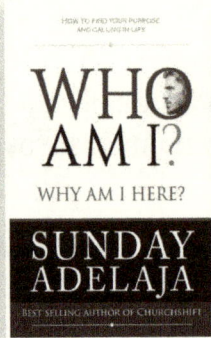

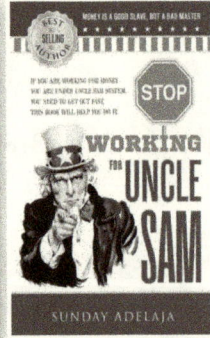

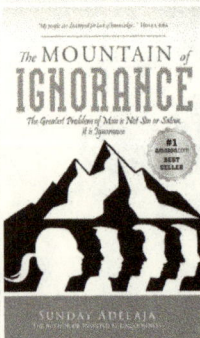

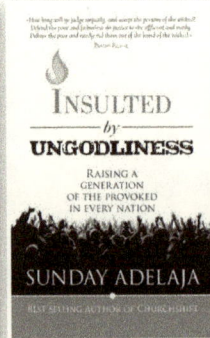

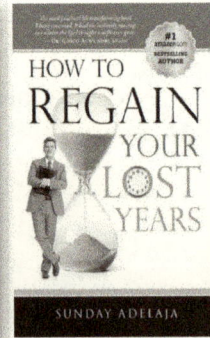

MONEY WON'T make you Rich
GOD'S PRINCIPLES FOR TRUE WEALTH, PROSPERITY, AND SUCCESS
SUNDAY ADELAJA

"IF NIGERIA DOES NOT SUCCEED, WHO ELSE CAN SUCCEED?"
— PETER ESHO, TRANSPARENCY INTERNATIONAL (GERMANY)
NIGERIA AND THE LEADERSHIP QUESTION
PROFFERING SOLUTIONS TO NIGERIA'S LEADERSHIP PROBLEM
SUNDAY ADELAJA
BEST SELLING AUTHOR OF CHURCHSHIFT

MYLES MUNROE
... FINDING ANSWERS TO WHY GOOD PEOPLE DIE TRAGIC AND EARLY DEATHS
SUNDAY ADELAJA

THE KINGDOM DRIVEN LIFE
Thy Kingdom Come, Thy will be Done on Earth . . .
SUNDAY ADELAJA
BEST SELLING AUTHOR OF CHURCHSHIFT

CHURCH SHIFT
SUNDAY ADELAJA

WHO AM I? WHY AM I HERE?
SUNDAY ADELAJA
BEST SELLING AUTHOR OF CHURCHSHIFT

ONLY GOD can save NIGERIA: What a Myth!
SUNDAY ADELAJA
The Author of Nigeria and the Leadership Question

MONEY IS A GOOD SLAVE, BUT A BAD MASTER
BEST SELLING AUTHOR
STOP WORKING FOR UNCLE SAM
SUNDAY ADELAJA

The MOUNTAIN of IGNORANCE
The Greatest Problem of Man is Not Sin or Satan, it is Ignorance
#1 AMAZON.COM BEST SELLER
SUNDAY ADELAJA

OLORUNWA

INSULTED by UNGODLINESS
RAISING A GENERATION OF THE PROVOKED IN EVERY NATION
SUNDAY ADELAJA
BEST SELLING AUTHOR OF CHURCHSHIFT

#1 AMAZON.COM BESTSELLING AUTHOR
HOW TO REGAIN YOUR LOST YEARS
SUNDAY ADELAJA

Best Selling Books by Dr. Sunday Adelaja
Available on Amazon.com and Okadabooks.com

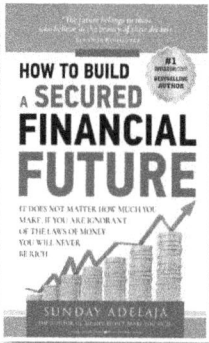

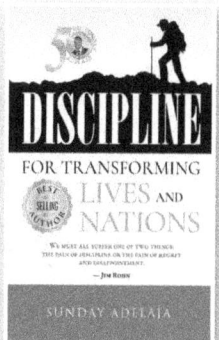

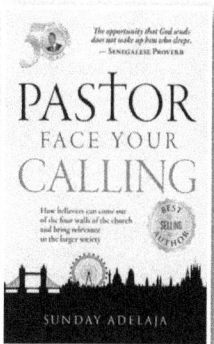

GOLDEN JUBILEE SERIES BOOKS
BY DR. SUNDAY ADELAJA

FOR DISTRIBUTION OR TO ORDER BULK COPIES OF THIS BOOKS, PLEASE CONTACT US:

USA | CORNERSTONE PUBLISHING
E-mail: info@thecornerstonepublishers.com, +1 (516) 547-4999
www.thecornerstonepublishers.com

AFRICA | SUNDAY ADELAJA MEDIA LTD.
E-mail: btawolana@hotmail.com
+2348187518530, +2348097721451, +2348034093699

LONDON, UK | PASTOR ABRAHAM GREAT
E-mail: abrahamagreat@gmail.com, +447711399828, +441908538141

KIEV, UKRAINE |
E-mail: pa@godembassy.org, Mobile: +380674401958